# Time Traveler's Bible

Written By

Timothy R. McBride

This writing is dedicated to the late Robert E. McBride. A man who devoted his life into the research of biblical philosophy, and organic gardening, and all the while teaching us all to think outside the box, yet questioning everything, while seeking the truth. Thank You ! " Pops " Rest In Peace

Copyright © 2020 by Timothy R. McBride

All rights reserved. This book or any portion thereof may not be reproduced or used in any manner whatsoever without the express written permission of the publisher except for the use of brief quotations in a book review or scholarly journal.

First Printing: 2020

Lulu Press, Inc.

627 Davis Drive, Suite 300,

Morrisville, NC 27560

ISBN 978-1-67817-973-1

# Time Traveler's Bible

0 - Fact or Fantasy.................................................................................. 6

1 - Hidden in plain sight.............................................................................7

2 - Revelation 2020 ...................................................................................9

3 - Good People, can still be bad humans ................................................14

4 – Antichrist ...........................................................................................17

5 - The Rapture .......................................................................................24

6 - Ten Commandments .........................................................................30

7 - Destruction of Jerusalem 70 AD.........................................................35

8 - Crucifixion A Hoax..............................................................................38

9 - The 144,000 ......................................................................................44

10 - Mark OF The Beast .........................................................................47

11 - Ancient Books And Fake News .......................................................54

12 - Earthling Hominoidea Sapien Solhumatan Terrarius.......................59

13 - Enochville of Nodium ................................................................................61

14 - The Beginning- Undeifying Creation ....................................................63

15 - A Border Less Planet ............................................................................65

16 - Why Colonizing the Moon Is A Bad Idea .............................................69

17 - Solar Energy Equals Freedom .............................................................74

18 - Altered Timeline ....................................................................................77

19 - Humans are attempting AI Future .......................................................78

20 - Its Alive ..................................................................................................78

22 - All encompassing..................................................................................79

## Fact or Fantasy

It is amazing how the populations of humans continue to choose fantasy over truth when it comes to religions, holidays, news, even science in the case of pseudoscience, but one modern phenomena sums it all up pretty well. That is the phenomena of the motion picture industry, where as since the advent of movies many human stories are now told on film. One aspect of this invention is that each story gets retold almost like clockwork with each generation or when new technology allows for a more dramatic demonstration of the story line but with many added effects or writer's twist on the story. What we get in the end is a wonderful retelling of the original story but slightly different if not dramatically different than the author's original works.

This action has been going on with each generation since the very invention of writing and humans began keeping stories and records as what we have before us today are works that have been revised hundreds of times, as well translated into many languages that totally lose most of the original content through terminology deficiencies.

The human species are story tellers and that is one talent our species does best. The trouble with some ancient stories after being handed all the way down to modern times is people still attempt to interpret them as literal when the truth is actually most of the ancients wrote using metaphors within mythology. A general rule of thumb is if the stories content does not actually exist within nature then it is a myth totally fiction as with the term supernatural implies. Although some actual history is being recorded it takes on a whole different genre by style and is easy recognizable. So take your time when studying, do the research, know what you are reading in time, space, place, and context, for everything that is real is still out there right before your very eyes.

## Hidden In Plain Sight

There are clues within scripture that usually fly right over the heads of most researchers. Nevertheless they are all there in plain sight. To get right into the meat of this writing,will list a few of these such scriptures with the highlights noted for your pondering mind to consider with some additional comments.

### Revelation 11:18

" The nations were angry, and your wrath has come. The time has come for judging the dead, and for rewarding your servants the prophets and your people who revere your name, both great and small-- and for destroying those who destroy the earth."

Okay most people do not even notice that last snip-it at the end of this scripture,

" and for destroying those who destroy the earth "

Ask yourself who is destroying the earth? Most people believe that this scripture refers to when Jesus Christ comes back at the end of the age with his angels to save, or reward the righteous followers within some religion or church, but look closer that is not what is being said at all. Now ask yourself,

" Who are the people not destroying the earth? "

Those who revere the natural earth and seek to save our planet in the name of the Elohim of Eden. ( A invisible spirit within all lifeforms)

## Hosea 4:6

" My people are destroyed from lack of knowledge. " Because you have rejected knowledge, I also reject you as my priests; because you have ignored the law of your God, I also will ignore your children. "

Okay notice the first part of this scripture,

" My people are destroyed from lack of knowledge."

Ask any so called Christian, they are always all on about knowing Jesus Christ yet according to this they are being destroyed because they don't know the God in question here, not being saved. Who has priest? Religions right? Seems this is saying the priest are being rejected ?

Seems the Elohim of Eden with the natural ways of living upon this earth is what is being forgotten so therefore the blessings are disappearing from our religious cultures, and their cities like a whirlwind. And what is this knowledge that people lack? This knowledge is the knowings of how to live with this earth in peace for all eternity with all life upon it.  To live with nature not destroying nature as eating from the tree of life and living forever.

## Exodus 20:4-6

" You shall not make for yourself an image in the form of anything in heaven above or on the earth beneath or in the waters below. You shall not bow down to them or worship them; for I, the Lord your God, am a jealous God, punishing the children for the sin of the parents to the third and fourth generation of those who hate me, but showing love to a thousand generations of those who love me and keep my commandments. "

Okay, one of the ten commandments but look again at what is actually being said here, No image worship period implies that the God in question here is of spirit and not an image at all. All religions that bow down to worship something are false idolatrous religions. Now think about DNA hereditary disease, those that run in the family, basically handed down from your parents. Okay a generation according to ancient text is 40 years basically the childbearing years of the average human female.

So we are talking up to 160 years to allow these defects to leave a bloodline with rectified living practices involved to correct some of these deficiencies in DNA. But on the other hand people with good genes from their parents as we say usually have much greater lifespans with way less disease yet according to this we are talking 40,000 years. What is being loved or hated here? Basically the dietary consumption set forth within the human body, including thoughts, that feeds the natural spirit within all humans.

That old saying, " You are what you eat ? " Hits way closer to home than you could of ever imagined. We human beings have at least 40,000 years to live on this planet at large with current DNA infrequence exposed to light energy from beyond and the light is good.

## Luke 17:21

" No one will say, 'Look, here it is!' or, 'There it is!'; because the Kingdom of God is within you."

All the people on this planet waiting for a God to return to establish a kingdom, or going to some heavenly place after death, or nations forming governments, or people forming religions are all missing the whole boat here. According to this scripture the Kingdom of God is here always within your living body already as truly we are all the collective temple of our living Elohim, " Thy" Elohim the Spirit God within you. We are all born into heaven as we begin to cherish the garden of Eden thriving within our souls.

## Revelation 2020

Have you ever wondered why, Revelation starts out by naming seven assembles of Israelite that had escaped the destruction of Judea by Rome, and are now refugees in the province of Asia? Well these are some of the 144,000 gathered from the twelve tribes of Israel that are now scattered northward evading away from the Roman Army escaping the fate of those that didn't heed the warnings of Yahshua the Messiah and others.

## Revelations 1, 9-11-

" I, John, your brother and companion in the suffering and kingdom and patient endurance that are ours in Yahshua, was on the island of Patmos because of the word of Yahweh and the testimony of Yahshua. On the Sabbath, I was in the Spirit, and I heard behind me a loud voice like a trumpet, which said: "Write on a scroll what you see and send it to the seven assemblies: to Ephesus, Smyrna, Pergamum, Thyatira, Sardis, Philadelphia and Laodicea."

John was exiled on the island of Patmos after being captured by the Romans so he had to cloak his letters in a code like form to conceal the messages in case the Romans confiscated the messages, so there is a lot of nonsensical rhetoric involved in the script, along with some added jargon to confuse otherwise. Then you have to decipher out all the crap that the mistranslators added in over the centuries mostly deliberate as well to get a handle on what the original was intended to relay.

" Look, he is coming with the clouds," and "every eye will see him, even those who pierced him"

This is the first clue within the text to let the readers know this message is for those Israelite who fled to Asia only. As likewise they had seen Yahshua leave them and go into the mountains to scout a path above the cloud line so now he has already returned from the clouds to lead the 144,000 gathered to safety, so of course they all saw him, even the guys that had pierced Yahshua was now among them as followers, placing this event in the 1st century during their lifetimes only.

After this John begins to describe throughout to them that didn't know the outcome because they had already left the area, the great holocaust that had just happened to Judea, over the period of the siege to the end of the War with Rome. The total destruction of the Kingdom of Judea, Jerusalem, and the Hebrew Temple. Included before all was lost then Chapter 7 the Manifest Of Yahshua to gather up the 144,000.

## Revelation 7, 3-8

" Do not harm the land or the sea or the trees until we put a seal on the foreheads of the servants of Yahweh our Elohim." Then I heard the number of those who were sealed: 144,000 from all the tribes of Israel. ( Simply meaning get these folks out of the region before the great war with Rome begins) From the tribe of Judah 12,000 were sealed, from the tribe of Reuben 12,000, from the tribe of Gad 12,000, from the tribe of Asher 12,000, from the tribe of Naphtali 12,000, from the tribe of Manasseh 12,000, from the tribe of Simeon 12,000, from the tribe of Levi 12,000, from the tribe of Issachar 12,000, from the tribe of Zebulun 12,000, from the tribe of Joseph 12,000, from the tribe of Benjamin 12,000 "

## Revelation 12, 1-3 "

"A great sign appeared in heaven: a woman clothed with the sun, with the moon under her feet and a crown of twelve stars on her head. She was pregnant and cried out in pain as she was about to give birth "

The women symbolically is the 144,000 being birthed (THE LAMB) with the 12 tribes under her care. The bit about the Moon, and the Sun lets the reader know that they are out away from civilization with nothing but the Moon, Sun and Stars above them.

## Revelation 12, 6

" The woman fled into the wilderness to a place prepared for her by Yahweh, where she might be taken care of for 1,260 days. "

Okay the 144,000 escaped with their savior Yahshua before the War with Rome had turned into a siege to a secret location in the wilderness away from civilization. The 1,260 day marker here was very important to the Israelite gathering for it set the time frame till moment in time the further Exodus would begin so as to not get left behind. A group from a tribe would need to assemble before this period. Just as today a group meeting to catch a jet, or a train to travel as a group to another location with a guide the date, and departure time is very important. After this John begins describing what happened to the people that remained in Judea as the End of Days for that world is completed, as he talks about the Beast. ( Roman Emperors)

**Revelations 13, 16-18**

" It ( The Roman Emperor -Beast ) also forced all people, great and small, rich and poor, free and slave, to receive a mark on their right hands or on their foreheads, so that they could not buy or sell unless they had the mark, which is the name of the beast or the number of its name. This calls for wisdom. Let the person who has insight calculate the number of the beast, for it is the number of a man. That number is 666."

So the Israelite left were either killed or reduced to slaves for the mighty Roman Empire, as it states here, all were stripped of their former station in life, and marked as slaves with brands or tattoos. All this began happening in the Year Of the Beast 66-6th (DCLXVI) Year-Month AD. A date that also coincidences with the archives within actual Roman History.

Enter - Josephus (a personal witness to the events) claims that over 1,100,000 people were killed during the initial siege, of which a majority were Jewish. 97,000 were captured and enslaved, and many fled to areas around the Mediterranean. Titus reportedly refused to accept a wreath of victory, as there is "no merit in vanquishing people forsaken by their own God." During the siege, there was mass starvation in which cannibalism widely occurred with, it is believed, some mothers even devouring their own children. Later, there were even mass crucifixions to the degree that wood eventually became unavailable. But the number of calamities which everywhere fell upon the nation at that time; the extreme misfortunes to which the inhabitants of Judea were especially subjected, the thousands of men, as well as women and children, that perished by the sword, by famine, and by other forms of death innumerable—all these things, as well as the many great sieges which were carried on against the cities of Judea, and the excessive sufferings endured by those that fled to Jerusalem itself, as to a city of perfect safety, and finally the general course of the whole war, as well as its particular occurrences in detail, and how at last the abomination of desolation, proclaimed by the prophets, Daniel 9:27 stood in the very temple of God, so celebrated of old, the temple which was now awaiting its total and final destruction by fire — all these things any one that wishes may find accurately described in the history written by Josephus.

**Matthew 24:21**

" For then there will be a great tribulation, such as has not occurred since the beginning of Judea until now, nor ever will."

Yahshua predicting what Josephus witnessed.

**Revelation 14**

" Then I looked, and there before me was the Lamb, standing on Mount Zion, and with him 144,000 who had his name and his Father's name written on their foreheads. And I heard a sound from heaven like the roar of rushing waters and like a loud peal of thunder. The sound I heard was like that of harpists playing their harps. And they sang a new song before the throne and before the four living creatures and the elders. No one could learn the song except the 144,000 who had been redeemed from Judea. These are those who did not defile themselves with women, for they remained pure. They follow the Lamb wherever he goes. They were purchased from among Israel and offered as first fruits to Yahweh and the Lamb. No lie was found in their mouths; they are blameless. "

Of course the best people, young mostly under age twenty five fit in mind and spirit for the riggers of the hard journey ahead north were chosen.

**Revelation 12, 13-17**

" When the dragon ( Roman Army) saw that he had been hurled to the earth, he pursued the woman ( 144,000) who had given birth to the male child. The woman ( 144,000) was given the two wings of a great eagle, so that she might fly to the place prepared for her in the wilderness, where she would be taken care of for a time, times and half a time, out of the serpent's ( Roman Army's) reach. Then from his ( Emperor's )mouth the serpent ( Roman Army) spewed water like a river, to overtake the woman ( 144,000) and sweep her away with the torrent. But the earth helped the woman ( 144,000) by opening its mouth and swallowing the river that the dragon ( Rome) had spewed out of his( Emperor's) mouth. Then the dragon ( Roman Army) was enraged at the woman( 144,000) and went off to wage war against the rest of her offspring—those who keep Yahweh's commands and hold fast their testimony about Yahshua."

Here is a very clear explanation of the exodus of the 144,000 Israelite from the Judean Region whom escaped the grasp of the Roman Army that was pursuing them. Some of the elite of the Roman Ruler-ship wanted to totally wipe the Israelite off the face of the earth with total genocide, and completely do away with the people and the religion. As a result of this decree many early Yahwish were murdered, by war, crucifixion, or in the Colosseum.

So this is confirmation that the 144,000 did indeed escape intact and are now traveling north into Asia towards their promised land and beyond some eventually sailing and settling within the British isles, and several other islands at the then edge of the known world. The last few chapters of Revelation are talking about the promise with a lot of wishful dreaming to give the refugees hope. A new start of a New Kingdom , that will be founded someday in a new land somewhere, a new world, where Eden can begin again with a chance at a new paradise. Many of these very peoples soon developed into the many European Nations we know today and later many of their descendants did sail to a New World, - A New York, A New Jersey, A New Jerusalem later to be known as America.

" And from the time the daily sacrifice is abolished and the abomination of desolation set up, there will be 1,290 days. Blessed is he who waits and reaches the end of the 1,335 days. But as for you, go on your way until the end. You will rest, and will arise to your inheritance at the end of the days."…

## Matthew 24 -

" So when you see standing in the holy place 'the abomination of desolation,' described by the prophet Daniel (let the reader understand), then let those who are in Judea flee to the mountains. Let no one on the housetop come down to retrieve anything from his house. And let no one in the field return for his cloak. How miserable those days will be for pregnant and nursing mothers! Pray that your flight will not occur in the winter or on the Sabbath. For at that time there will be great tribulation, unmatched from the beginning of the Judea until now, and never to be seen again. If those days had not been cut short, nobody would be saved. But for the sake of the elect, those days will be cut short. At that time, if anyone says to you, 'Look, here is the Messiah!' or 'There He is,' do not believe it. For false Messiahs and false prophets will appear and perform great signs and wonders that would deceive even the elect, if that were possible. See, I have told you in advance. "

## Good People, can still be bad humans

This has nothing to do with natural habitats but perspective only . The word Good, or Bad is lost within the human idea of religion or social status, and or success or failure with money. What really does it mean by saying someone is a " Good " Christian, or a " Bad " Scientist, or visa versa? One has to do with one's concept of morality within a Universe controlled by a God, whereas the other may deal with scientific evidence, or theory within a Godless Universe. Either way, both concepts only exist within the minds of humans with a single conscience that has both thoughts of good and bad, truth or illusion. One's nationality is simply a birthright within one's culture of origin.

## Mark 10:18

"Why do you call me good?" Yahshua answered. "No one is good--except Yahweh ( God) alone.

**Genesis 2**- Narrates metaphorically that Yahweh places man and woman in a garden with trees of whose fruits they may eat, but forbids them to eat from "the tree of the knowledge of good and evil."
On the one hand you have evil- crimes, drugs, rape, war, and pollution, while on the other hand you have good people gone bad making bad decisions as if a split personality. God demands us to not think of neither. Both are forbidden so therefore no division between them exist. Whereas Science is either good, or bad yet awaits disapproval or acceptance by human cultures, as reality or fantasy. In the end there is no difference except what you hold dear within your own heart and mind. One man's good can be another man's bad just as one man's trash may become another man's treasure. Turning billions of human beings to believe in a false " Messiah "created by " Rome" while screaming from their Catholic " Book" inside millions of buildings with billions of cars parked outside is not the way to Heaven. Now they ( Climate Scientist) say all these cars have helped cause " Global Warming" sounds like, " Hell " to me.  Now add the Cult of Football Stadiums to the equation as the waste and energy exponentially destroys a planetary ecosystem in exchange for fun & games, false religions, monetary gain, and meaningless repetitive holidays. Religion ( See 10 Commandments ) is only needed if one does not know how to behave with his neighbors otherwise.

Sad that it has to come to ritual inside buildings instead of a way of life with a planet and it's trillions of species. ( Tree of Life) If you are reading and teaching people from a book any book ritually then it is a false religion, because the only true religion on this earth is to know, and love and respect nature, outdoors- " Here & Now "

Humans are Humans are Humans. There are no labels, or separations just illusions and tons of paperwork, and uniforms that attempts to explain separations of religions, governments, and corporations, but at the end of the day just humans. Brainwashed from their own human nature, while mostly living within man made mega metropolitan creations that continually expand while bulldozing the natural habitats for so called manifest destiny, eminent domain, and monetary progress.

**Matthew 7:13**

"You ( The few Thousands ) can enter Creator Yahweh's Natural Spirit Kingdom ( Eden) only through the narrow gate. The highway to destruction is broad, and its gate is wide for the many ( Billions) who choose that way.

**Revelation 22:1-3**

" Then the messenger ( Time Traveler) showed me a river of the water of life, as clear as crystal, ( Pollution of Earth's life sustaining systems has ended) flowing from the throne of Yahweh (Natural Spirit Creator Being) and of the Lamb ( Nation Healers) down the middle of the main street of New Yahrusalem, ( Future Human Sustainable Biospherian Habitat) On either side of the river stood a tree of life, bearing twelve kinds of fruit and yielding a fresh crop for each month. And the leaves of the tree are for the healing of the nations. "

Sad when you realize there is no such thing as a so called" Holy Land " for all of our beloved Earth is sacred. All forms of ritualized organized religion is not only evil but false to it's very core and to imagine all the deaths for these empty causes over the many millennia is madness. The very book that spawn such madness speaks of a " NEW " Jerusalem, not of this current world, yet these poor foolish souls died fighting for the old city of symbolic Babylon herself, and to think this madness still persists as the fight continues thousands of years later between the great religions of the world. Amazing how a single lie whispered in the dead of night can still dominate a world full of ignorant human primates so desperately seeking a savior. A savior from what? I guess themselves.

# Antichrist

**Setting 1st Century C. E -**

**John 4: 1-3 -**

" Beloved, do not trust every spirit but test the spirits to see whether they belong to Yahweh, because many false prophets have gone out into the world. This is how you can know the Spirit of Yahweh: every spirit that acknowledges Yahshua the Messiah come in the flesh ( Son of Man with natural human parents) belongs to Yahweh and every spirit that does not acknowledge does not belong to Yahweh.
" This is the spirit of the Anti-Messiah ( Immaculate virgin birth GOD/Man Antichrist ) that, as you heard, is to come, but in fact is already in the world."

Many Authors and biblical researchers place the Antichrist into our future when in fact no where in bibles anywhere can you find this idea, but instead what few scriptures that mention the Antichrist or correctly translated False Messiah, or False Prophet was already in the world during the first century. The key to understanding this is knowing what the word " Spirit " meant to the original authors.

Spirit was used to describe a thought within the human mind that one holds as an idea either false, real, or imagined, as is basically how the word is defined today. Hence if someone is said to, have a bad, or evil spirit, that would mean that that soul has been corrupted with wrong thoughts, or ideas. Furthermore the human spirit is said to be the nonphysical part of a person which is the seat of emotions and character; the soul, ( Spirit ) those qualities regarded as forming the definitive or typical elements in the character of a person, nation, or group or in the thought and attitudes of a particular period, a person identified with their most prominent mental or moral characteristics or with their role in a group or movement. Another good modern way to explain this concept is to think of the human brain as the hardware and the human spirit as the software loaded into the human mind or CPU and just as a computer can become corrupted, hacked, full of viruses, fake news, illusions, lies, false information, or just bad programming so can the human spirit within. So the idea of the Anti-Christ which, " Christ " simply means Messiah, in the Greek language.

So think about it, what is being explained here is that we will have two ideas of a Messiah. One will be true the other False, or Anti as a belief system that is being taught among the people. When one looks into the first century you will find this to be true as one portion of the people believed Yahshua was the Messiah yet was fully human in every way with human parents very natural, whereas on the other hand you have this group of humans forming the belief that, Yahshua the Messiah ( Later translated as, Jesus Christ) was a supernatural GOD/Man borne from a Virgin Mother, which is idolatry in its purest form, and the average Hebrew never heard of this concept before, but this type belief was very common among the Roman elite of that same period as Mithraism, which is the new idea that, as you heard, is to come, but in fact is already in the world."

In Ancient Rome, religion was an integral part of the civil government. Beginning with the Roman Senate's declaration of the divinity of Julius Caesar on 1 January 42 BC. Emperors were proclaimed gods on Earth and demanded to be worshiped accordingly.

The real question is who is spreading these false teachings that are already there in the world 1st century ?

" This is the spirit of the Anti-Messiah ( Antichrist ) that, as you heard, is to come, but in fact is already in the world."

This was a warning sent out to the people listening to John speak in the 1st Century A.D. Of course this is John referring to the False Apostle Paul, that was already going about teaching this false doctrine, in their time, converting many people away from the original teachings of Yahshua, but instead forming what was the beginnings of Catholicism.

## Acts 1:12–26

" So one of the men who have accompanied us during all the time Yahshua went in and out among us, beginning from the baptism of John until the day when he was taken up ( Into the Mountains) from us—one of these men must become with us a witness to his resurrection. ( "raising up" or "standing up again, surviving a great ordeal " )

And they put forward two, Joseph called Barsabbas, who was also called Justus, and Matthias. And they prayed and said, "You, Elohim who know the hearts( Spirit) of all, show which one of these two you have chosen to take the place in this ministry and apostleship from which Judas turned aside to go to his own place.  And they cast lots for them, and the lot fell on Matthias, and he was numbered with the eleven apostles. "

There can only be twelve true Apostles so Matthias was appointed, after Judas to make the count twelve again. These twelve Yahshua sent out with the following instructions:

**Matthew 10: 5-7-**

"Do not go among the Gentiles or enter any town of the Samaritans. Go rather to the lost sheep of the tribes of Israel.  ( The 144,000 were to be gathered up for the exodus from Judea very quickly preserving a remnant before the war with Rome begins)  If anyone will not welcome you or listen to your words, leave that home or town and shake the dust off your feet. Truly I tell you, it will be more bearable for Sodom and Gomorrah on the day of judgment than for that town.  ( The Israeli town's people that did not heed the call and got out, were in fact totally destroyed by the roman army and burnt to the ground )  I tell you the truth, you will not finish going through the cities of Israel before the Son of Man comes." ( Yahshua coming to lead the 144,000 collected as commanded to gather, to safety in the wilderness. )

False Apostle Paul ( Saul) was self- appointed, never walked with Yahshua the Messiah ever, and never witnessed the true real Living Messiah among the tribes of Israel ever, so this fact alone identifies Paul as the impostor, who in fact did the opposite as requested by Yahshua, also his writings were all added later superimposed cleverly into the writings of Roman Catholic Holy Bibles that were orchestrated into, The Emperor's Christ at the Council of Nicaea, under the guidance of Emperor Constantine.

**Acts 9:19-22**

" and after taking some food, he regained his strength. Saul ( Paul ) spent several days with the disciples  in Damascus. At once he began to preach in the synagogues that Yahshua is the Son of God.  All those who heard him were astonished and asked, "Isn't he the man who raised havoc in Jerusalem among those who call on this name?  And hasn't he come here to take them as prisoners to the chief priests?"

Here Paul began teaching that Yahshua is the Son Of God, not the Son Of Man which was the term that Yahshua himself always told people to address him as for fear that people would begin to worship him thus creating idolatry.

So the so called, Antichrist is just a belief system not a actual man, or any form of a man, or a god, supernatural being, or any other likeness otherwise. But instead a false religious cult movement that was beginning in the world during the first century, and that movement later became what we all have been handed down to become known as modern Christianity which has basically changed everything Yahshua actually taught and believed yet instead established Sunday worship along with every pagan holiday on the, Gregorian calendar one could ever imagine to galore.

**Matthew 5: 17-18**

" In the same way, let your light shine before men, that they may see your good deeds and glorify your Father in heaven. Do not think that I have come to abolish the Law or the Prophets; I have not come to abolish them, but to fulfill them. I tell you truly, until heaven and earth pass away, not a single jot, not a stroke of a pen, will disappear from the Law until everything is accomplished.…"

Of course Yahshua was talking about the Old Testament and the Ten Commandments because the New Testament hasn't even been written yet at this time.. To fulfill a law simply means to keep it as a living standard for your life.( In other words its in your DNA, it is your HARD DRIVE)

" Until everything is accomplished "

This simply means that this law will stay in effect until a true Kingdom Of Heaven is established on Earth in which every single earthly citizen becomes law abiding, and also fulfills their life with righteous deeds instead of evil and wicked deeds.
A few other places where the word " Antichrist " is used in the bibles are listed here with comments, as John was writing to his friends in his day about the news of the day that was happening at that time as Judea was being invaded and finally totally destroyed by the Roman Army, all occurred in the 1st century time frame.

**1 John 2: 18-19**

" Dear children, this is the last hour; and as you have heard that the antichrist is coming, even now many Antichrists have come. This is how we know it is the last hour. They went out from us, but they did not really belong to us. For if they had belonged to us, they would have remained with us; but their going showed that none of them belonged to us. "

Imagine the alert or news flash of the day's headline read---

" THIS IS THE LAST HOUR ! "
( End of Days )

Imagine a message coming to you telling you that the Roman Army is about to invade your nation and that your world is about to be totally destroyed. No wonder many people of those days thought of Nero Emperor of Rome the first, Antichrist - Beast especially after his General Titus Flavius Vespasianus totally destroyed the Jewish Temple just as predicted setting the stage for the False Christ Religion to emerge and the abomination of desolation to begin starting with the desecration of the Hebrew Temple by Titus by sacrificing a bull, a sheep, and a pig to the Roman Gods as people even previously were already defecting to the Roman side pleading allegiance for fear of their lives. Meantime you can get a sense of the division already in the works as people begin to splinter, from ideas that had held them together for millennia to this whole new religious mentality.

**2 John 1:6-8**

" And this is love, that we walk according to His ( Yahweh's) commandments. This is the very commandment you have heard from the beginning, that you must walk in love. For many deceivers have gone out into the world, refusing to understand the coming of Yahshua the Messiah in the flesh. ( Son of Man fully human in every way ) Any such person is the deceiver and the Antichrist.( GOD/Man Anti- Human )  Watch yourselves, so that you do not lose what we have worked for, that you may be fully saved "

This message also was sent out warning the Children of Israel of that time that false messiahs were coming and not to be deceived, but instead hold fast, for the real Messiah will return with a pathway out of this disaster otherwise pending as a very urgent national emergency.
Yahshua speaking to his followers of that generation 1st Century only -

**Matthew 24: 15-25**

" So when you see standing in the holy place ( Jewish Temple At Jerusalem ) 'the abomination that causes desolation, ( Roman Armies) spoken of through the prophet Daniel—let the reader understand— then let those who are in Judea flee to the mountains. Let no one on the housetop go down to take anything out of the house. Let no one in the field go back to get their cloak. How dreadful it will be in those days for pregnant women and nursing mothers! Pray that your flight will not take place in winter or on the Sabbath. For then there will be great distress, unequaled from the beginning of Judea until now—and never to be equaled again. If those days had not been cut short, no one would survive, but for the sake of the elect ( 144,000 that fled ) those days will be shortened. At that time if anyone says to you, 'Look, here is the Messiah!' or, 'There he is!' do not believe it. For false messiahs and false prophets will appear and perform great signs and wonder to deceive, if possible, even the elect. See, I have told you ahead of time. "

Josephus, the Jewish historian who gives us the clearest first hand account of Jerusalem's fall, 70 CE reports that some people in Judea heeded Yahshua's warning. When the city and temple fell, more than one million Judeans died. But most true followers of Yahshua by and large, were not among them, for they had already fled the city when they saw the Romans coming, as forewarned to do, so were saved from this horrible fate.

It is amazing to think about the millions of people that actually believe these messages referring to the Antichrist have something to do with our time, 21st century or our future when actually any belief that places these messages into any other time than the first century natural earth setting is totally wrong, and ironically just as much as of an illusion as the people that were spreading the ideas of a false messiah religion in those days.

The only message that relates to our time is the keeping of the ten commandments, a message that the real actual great human teacher Yahshua the Messiah of his time taught would someday usher in a grand future world of true peace and prosperity like the human species has never known before, a place in time Yahshua coined the, Kingdom of Heaven.

**Mark 10:17-21**

As Yahshua was starting out on his way to Jerusalem, a man came running up to him, knelt down, and asked,

"Good Teacher, what must I do to inherit eternal life?

"Why do you call me good?" Yahshua asked. "Only Yahweh is truly good. But to answer your question, you know the commandments: 'You must not murder. You must not commit adultery. You must not steal. You must not testify falsely. You must not cheat anyone. Honor your father and mother. "

"Teacher," the man replied,

"I've obeyed all these commandments since I was young."

Looking at the man, Yahshua felt genuine love for him. There is still one thing you haven't done," he told him. "Go and sell all your possessions and give the money to the poor, and you will have treasure in heaven. "

Think about the wisdom in this, as the one commandment Yahshua didn't mention about human relations was, thou shall not covet, as the young man had way more than he needed yet was not willing to share with others so the people around him had become poor.

We still see a lot of this happening today so yes, here is a message for our times for sure. Think about it, you are selling all this excess stuff, you don't really need to other folks that can buy it, and meanwhile, you are helping the poorer with the proceeds.

## The Rapture

We are still finding it amazing how some Authors can find one tiny snip-it of ancient scripture, totally mistranslated, totally out of context yet will build this entire idea from that and sell it to the masses as truth. Take for instance the Rapture.. No where in Bibles, ancient or modern can one find this concept, or even the word yet we got millions of books sold, and now tons of movies all over on this subject that never even existed before in antiquity, or any archives of history anywhere. Now we got millions of people believing they are going to go flying off into the heaven, like some superman, Beam me up Scotty style Escape!

The theory of the Rapture comes from just a few very misinterpreted scripture,

Setting 1st Century AD Earth

**1 Thessalonians 4:17**

"Then we who are alive, who are left, will be caught up together with them above the clouds to meet Yahshua in the aire, and so we will always be with our savior, our guide. Therefore encourage one another with these words."

The Jews ( Year 67 AD ) that were facing the Roman Army were expecting a savior to come an rescue them from the approaching Roman armies. So this message was sent out as a reassurance for those still in Jerusalem during the coming seize,

" Then we who are alive, who are left. "

Those not killed by the initial Roman Army attacks on Jerusalem, will be, " caught up " ( Some modern interpreters falsely insert " raptures " here instead of, " caught up " but the bigger mistake is they put this setting into our future which is totally wrong ) together with them already above the mountain clouds into the open air to meet up with Yahshua and join as the 144,000 to flight away. Those that were already gathering up in the mountains of Judea fleeing from the Roman Army, the flight out away north escaping the massacre that was to come. So tell those that survived help is here but we must act fast to catch the Exodus from Jerusalem.

**Matthew 24:40-43,**

"At that time two men will be working in a field: one will be taken away, the other will be left behind. Two women will be at a mill grinding meal: one will be taken away, the other will be left behind. "Be on your guard, then, because you do not know what day Yahshua, will come.""

Taken here simply means killed or captured by the Roman Army, so be on your guard, don't miss the gathering up of refugees fleeing into the mountains above the clouds, at a special meeting place already prearranged once the attacks begin but that date is not known yet, only the Roman General Titus knew that date.

**Luke 21: 19-21**

" By your patient endurance, you will gain your souls. But when you see Jerusalem surrounded by armies, you will know that her desolation is near. Then let those who are in Judea flee to the mountains, let those in the city get out, and let those in the country stay out of the city."

A message to warn the People of Judea,( 70 AD ) and Jerusalem of that time, when the Roman Armies appear to surround the city, leave get out flea, or you will not survive. Many people heeded this call but also many didn't and were killed or taken captive by the Romans.

**Mark 13:14-23**

" So when you see standing in the holy place 'the abomination of desolation,'( Roman Armies of Emperor Nero year 66,6th Month, AD ) described by the prophet Daniel (let the reader understand), then let those who are in Judea flee to the mountains. Let no one on the housetop come down to retrieve anything from his house. And let no one in the field return for his cloak. How miserable those days will be for pregnant and nursing mothers! Pray that your flight will not occur in the winter or on the Sabbath. For at that time there will be great tribulation, unmatched from the beginning of the Kingdom of Judea, until now, and never to be seen again. If those days had not been cut short, nobody would be saved. But for the sake of the elect,(144,000 who escaped) those days will be cut short. "

It would not of been easy in those times to flea a marching Army at the magnitude of Rome, in those days especially if you were a woman with a child, or if the Romans decided to attack in the cold of winter, but you can get a sense of the emergency if one cannot even jump from his rooftop lookout once spotting the invasion, to even get a coat for the field, but instead run like hell.

" If those days had not been cut short, nobody would be saved. But for the sake of the elect, (144,000 who escaped with Yahshua) those days will be cut short."

In other words the total destruction and total annihilation of a Jewish people will not occur at this dispensation in time, because Yahshua, The Savior of Israel 70 AD - ahead of schedule went into the wilderness and prepared a place for his people..

**Matthew 10:23**

"When you are persecuted in one place, flee to another. I tell you the truth, you will not finish going through the cities of Israel before the Son of Man comes."

This was send out as a message sometime around year 65 AD about the gathering up of the 144,000 Israelites which was the manifest issued by Yahshua to preserve the tribes of Israel for future times, these numbers must be made ready for the Exodus from Judea. So before the messengers could get the word out to the Children of Israel, the War with Rome will begin so they had to act fast to save as many as possible that would heed the call..( We should also point out that the real Yahshua always referred to himself as " Son of Man" this was done so people would know that he was not to be worshiped, in which would be idolatry, but also lets people know that he comes from Man not a God, also to differentiate from the Antichrist spirit already in the world at that time which claimed to be borne from a virgin mother and was the Son of God.

**John 4: 1-3 -**

" Beloved, do not trust every spirit but test the spirits to see whether they belong to Yahweh, because many false prophets have gone out into the world. This is how you can know the Spirit of Yahweh: every spirit that acknowledges Yahshua the Messiah come in the flesh ( Son of Man with natural human parents) belongs to Yahweh and every spirit that does not acknowledge does not belong to Yahweh. This is the spirit of the Anti-Messiah ( Immaculate virgin birth GOD/Man Antichrist ) that, as you heard, is to come, but in fact is already in the world."

The Antichrist is another subject that is also very much mistaken as an future event when according to this passage the Antichrist was already there in the world first century.

**Acts 1:9-**

" After He had said this, they watched as He was taken up, and a mountain cloud hid Him from their sight. "Men of Galilee," they said, "why do you stand here looking into the clouds. This same Yahshua, who has been taken from you into the clouds will come back in the same way you have seen Him go into the cloud." Then they returned to Jerusalem from the Mount of Olives, which is near the city, a Sabbath day's journey away. "

So Yahshua with his men left the area to go into the wilderness with his men to scout out a path, to take with the 144,000 thousand that was being gathered up from the tribes of Israel. There was not much room for error as this pathway which had to be well explored as a safe secure passage, that would evade the Roman Armies. Yahshua's men reassured the Men of Galilee that had the commission to get this message out quickly, and that they would return to the mountains around Judea in so much time to meet up with the 144,000 that was to be gathered up among all tribes of Israel for the Exodus.

**Revelation 1: 1-3**

" The revelation of Yahshua the Messiah, which Wisdom gave him to show to his followers the things that must soon take place. He made it known by sending messengers to his followers. John, who bore witness to the word of Yahweh, and to the testimony of Yahshua the Messiah, even to all that he saw. Blessed is the one who reads aloud the words of this before warning, and blessed are those who hear, and who heed what is written in it, for the time is near."

This was a High Alert Warning, sent out to the followers of Yahshua during the first century that were dealing with the dilemma of their time against the Roman Occupation and, Impending Invasion. So all these things in Revelation must, " soon" take place, for the time is, " near " Yahshua knew ahead of time that the Romans would attack and massacre Jerusalem, and the Kingdom of Judea would end very soon during that current century, so he developed a plan to save some of his people from each tribe of Israel from this horrible fate.

This message was only meant for the people living at that time in the 1st century as the text states and is addressed to them only, for the, " Time is near. " The End of Days, for the Kingdom of Judea, not thousands of years later, or any other generation.

**Matthew 24:34**

" Verily I say unto you, This generation shall not pass, till all these things be fulfilled "

**Matthew 16:28**

" Truly I tell you, some who are standing here will not taste death before they see the Son of Man coming to gather the 144,000 elect "

These statements are proof that Yahshua was talking to that generation only, ( 1st Century ) meaning the people that were actually alive at that time, will not die before all these things will happen in their generation, not some future generation.

**Revelation 7:4-8**

" And I heard the number of them which were sealed: and there were sealed an hundred and forty and four thousand of all the tribes of the children of Israel. Of the tribe of Juda were sealed twelve thousand. Of the tribe of Reuben were sealed twelve thousand. Of the tribe of Gad were sealed twelve thousand. Of the tribe of Aser were sealed twelve thousand. Of the tribe of Nephthalim were sealed twelve thousand. Of the tribe of Manasses were sealed twelve thousand. Of the tribe of Simeon were sealed twelve thousand. Of the tribe of Levi were sealed twelve thousand. Of the tribe of Issachar were sealed twelve thousand. Of the tribe of Zabulon were sealed twelve thousand. Of the tribe of Joseph were sealed twelve thousand. Of the tribe of Benjamin were sealed twelve thousand. And I looked, and, lo, a Lamb stood on the mount Sion, and with him an hundred forty and four thousand, "

This is the record sent out of the success, confirmation of the gathering up of the Israelite people to escape the Roman Army as they met all together on the Mountains of Judea, with Yahshua, their guide, and true savior of his people fleeing into the wilderness together as the Exodus from Judea begins, thus surviving the whole ordeal intact for future migrations of the tribes of Israel, which later grew into the many far northern European Nations far beyond the reach of the Mighty Roman Empire, and later as promised a NEW WORLD called America.

**21st Century C. E. Earth..**

It is somewhat ironic that each generation of translators, and revisers over the centuries have all doctored these writings, books, and letters between a few teachers, authors, and messengers from the 1st century that were just basically sending coded messages between themselves trying to figure a way out of a horrible mess they found themselves in as a conquered people. Seems though they always get re-translated in some form to suit whatever dogmatic doctrine being ritualized at the time, but none have doctored them as much as the current generation of writers now living, except maybe the Romans themselves that changed, altered, inserted, contrived, added to, twisted, and mistranslated, these testaments to form their mighty Roman Catholic Church of total paganism, from the Mithra holidays, to Anti-Christ/Sun-god worship of down right idolatry, sprinkled with every kind of voodoo, hocus, pocus, mumbo, jumbo, un-natural thing one could imagine from the walking dead, to Halloween tricks, before the Birth of the SUN, Day, December 25th. A brand new religion with all of Satan's hell, angels, demons, devils, ghosts, spirits, saints, virgin goddess, idols, witches, gods, bishops, priest, and popes to boot. Yet, as most historians agree, the winning side of any war will rewrite the history to suit their beliefs, instead of the dismayed, and conquered.

The Roman totally wrecked Judea, along with their religion, and temple in the first century, then they resurrected a similar religion with a new temple in Rome called the Vatican with a brand new resurrected Demigod they later coined, Jesus Christ. The Roman Catholic Christianity has been their cash cow for so long now that the few within it's ranks that diligently search and find the truth will still not relinquish the illusion, for fear of ridicule, such is the peer pressure that it is in their DNA herd mentality.

Yet, amazingly one can still find the truth about the real Savior of his world : Yahshua the Messiah, just by placing these text into proper context, without all the pseudo, but instead with the proper 1st century setting, then they light up, and begin to make sense. " All together as with any part of actual history one can learn a lesson for all human generations, as the human condition still remains basically the same throughout all ages, but with time we do advance and evolve hopefully continually for the betterment of all mankind "

# Ten Commandments

Why modern governments, and religions will not accept the original ten commandments as the law of the land?
One the ten commandments would do away with all other forms of governments, and religions alike. The ten commandments are a self-governing system so naturally governments, and religions are against them. The ten commandments forbids any worship of forms, or images, or likenesses so that would do away with all known modern organized religions that are centered around the worship of some external image of a man, gods, demigods, prophets or messiahs. No where in bibles anywhere can you find the concept of, " Original Sin " simply does not exist, so here again another totally made up story.

So let us analyze these ten commandments to see the wisdom within them, as their unique power to transform life and community.

**Exodus 20**

1- " I am Yahweh thy Elohim, which have brought thee out of the land of Egypt, out of the house of bondage. Thou shalt have no other gods before me."

Keywords here is " house of bondage" and the simple little word called, " thy " Thy makes it personal, a individual, a single human being, thyself. House of bondage, means slavery, servitude, a slave to the system, taxes, labor, tithes ...etc. Thy, is where all this takes place within thine own mind is where freedom resides, and is the place where your Elo-Him ( Female/Male) spirit lives within you. Thy soul set free from bondage freeing of the god spirit within you as all other gods outside of this is idolatry a sin unto thyself. Yahweh means I AM- Of course I am that I am, we all are a true living breathing human being, I AM alive Thy living Spirit.

2- " Thou shalt not make unto thee any graven image, or any likeness of any thing that is in heaven above, or that is in the earth beneath, or that is in the water under the earth. Thou shalt not bow down thyself to them, nor serve them: for I, Yahweh thy Elohim am a jealous Elohim, visiting the iniquity of the fathers upon the children unto the third and fourth generation of them that hate me;And shewing mercy unto thousands of them that love me, and keep my commandments. "

Keywords here are image, likeness - not bow down, nor serve, anything in heaven or earth or the oceans of earth. Okay that does away with all known organized religions of humans on planet earth for the text says " Make unto thee, that individual again not a church or a organization as is referred, " Thyself " period. Okay next keyword is " generation " Generation ( Forty years is a generation basically the average child bearing years of the human female. ) Implies family, tribe, clan, ancestors, descendants, family tree, genetics, inheritance. Think about what is being stated here in the form of actions that can effect future generations of one's own offspring, repercussions of karma that exist between just two human emotions , love and hate, but look there is another emotion mentioned, jealousy. Consider a mind full of hate, or a mind full of love, or a mind full of jealousy? How does emotion effect your genes, health, vitality, and longevity ?

Seems here quite a bit as hate can effect your children for up to four generations, or 160 years, as well on the other hand love can effect your children for thousands of generations, or 40,000 years plus in a more positive direction. The jealousy just means the karma is steadfast, unforgiving, inevitable force within nature inside thy hereditary genealogy, that was passed onto you as you pass it down to your children after you, Thy Elohim.

**3-** "Thou shalt not take the name of Yahweh thy Elohim in vain; for Yahweh will not hold him guiltless that taketh his name in vain."

Okay this is serious business for, " Whatsoever a man soweth, that shall he also reap " You cannot escape karma, for every action has an equal and opposite reaction. What one puts inside your mind, and body is important, so program Thy Elohim for great success, and health and never take that responsibility in vain. So do away with all guilt and free your mind of sinful thoughts as soon as possible.

**4-** " Remember the sabbath day, to keep it holy. Six days shalt thou labour, and do all thy work: But the seventh day is the sabbath of Yahweh thy Elohim: in it thou shalt not do any work, thou, nor thy son, nor thy daughter, thy manservant, nor thy maidservant, nor thy cattle, nor thy stranger that is within thy gates: For in six epochs, Creator made heaven and earth, the sea, and all that in them is, and rested the seventh day: wherefore Yahweh blessed the sabbath day, and hallowed it. "

Human Beings need a day of rest, a day to dream and reflect time. It is a biological necessity and is needed to maintain good health both physically and mentally. The ancients knew this was very important so the tribes set aside a day of rest for all humans.

The original, sabbath's days were calculated by the Moon phases, as were rooted within the agriculturally based tribes living upon this earth under the stars, and migrating with the seasons. Nowadays the false religions of this world have hijacked the Sabbath days and have replaced them with empty rituals to false gods instead within churches, temples, synagogues, and mosque. So instead of " remembering " the sabbath days most have forgotten them.

**5-** " Honour thy father and thy mother: that thy days may be long upon the land which Yahweh thy Elohim giveth thee. "

Okay notice here," thy " Thy is used four times in this commandment as we all have a personal relation with our parents. Think about the ways we can honour our parents, and now think of ways we can dishonour our parents? We cannot choose our biological parents so their DNA got passed onto us wither we like it or not, but either way we can honour them for what, we have this life, and also a chance to make a better world for our offspring who follow. This commandment also comes with a promise of long life upon the land which is giveth thee. In other words your inheritance, your birthright. It is a shame as to how so many peoples have squandered their lands for debt, basically losing their family farms leaving nothing to be passed onto a new generation. Of course honour of the land takes on a whole new meaning as we humans become stewards with husbandry responsibilities for our natural kingdom that is both male and female in nature our Great Father & Mother, Earth & Sky.

**6-** " Thou shalt not kill. "

All humans that do not die of a natural death, of old age have been killed by something either war, or disease, or drugs, or accident whatever something has taken them before their time. This commandment does away with all war, and brings about total peace upon this ravaged, violated, mutilated, polluted planet. The concept here is so simple yet encompasses all.

**7-** " Thou shalt not commit adultery."

The dictionary defines adultery as infidelity, unfaithfulness, falseness, disloyalty, cuckoldry, extramarital sex; affair, liaison, fling, amour; carrying-on, hanky-panky, two-timing, a bit on the side, fooling around, playing around. Adultery can take on higher meanings such as adulteration of a planet. Not being truthful to a higher cause, lowering your guard, not being a good, " Adult! " Be responsible, faithful, and truthful with all your relationships regardless be honest.

**8-** "Thou shalt not steal."

Imagine a world without locks, open doors everywhere, such a honor system this would be. This simple little commandment could do away with all security systems, all alarms,all borders, and fear of robbery everywhere. What is stealing really? Is lands taken in a war stealing? Is taxing someone's income stealing? What is ours to steal? Our goods, our services, our land, our possessions , our birthright, our heritage, our labor, our health, our privacy ?  But the commandment is deeper it states Thou, Thy, You, shalt not steal. You can rob yourself of nutrition by eating junk food, you can rob yourself of many things stealing away the times of your life with foolishness, rituals and games.

**9-** " Thou shalt not bear false witness against thy neighbour."

To lie, create a deception, to be dishonest. To give a false account of a matter. Okay no one enjoys being lied to, but can you imagine a totally honest world where telling false statements have not been heard for thousands of years. The truth becomes the norms, no fake news, no false messiahs, no false gods, no false religions, false governments. Who is our neighbor? From a global perspective everything is our neighbor, every insect, every worm, every creature on the planet. From a local perspective neighbor is those that live close to you in your neighborhood for instance, and who would want to be labeled dishonest by the locals? No matter how hard truthfulness is always the best medicine.

**10-** " Thou shalt not covet thy neighbour's house, thou shalt not covet thy neighbour's wife, nor his manservant, nor his maidservant, nor his ox, nor his ass, nor any thing that is thy neighbour's."

Desire! What do you desire? To possess something starts within the mind as a want, a need a lust, a fantasy, a desire. To live together in communities we need a few ground rules and this one just about sums it all up. The easy way to look at this is to imagine what you do not covet. Are you contented with what you have? Satisfied, fulfilled, happy, or do you spend your days wanting something someone else has, until it becomes a obsession. More, More , More we live in this consumer world where more is better, the latest stuff we must have, now not later. The driver of most debt in the world is covertness, and the merchants know this that is why the media is blanketed with commercials, endless advertisements designed in a way to create that desire for the item, person, place, or thing. " Keeping up with the Joneses " Four car garage and we're still building on. Nations trying to be like other nations copy cats everywhere duplication a billion, be like them, walk like them, become them. Mass media covets, corporate takeovers, money madness, greed all comes from covetousness. Just do not do it. Train your mind otherwise, be tranquilly pleased.

" Live long and prosper! "

Looking at this moon calendar the Sabbaths would fall on the 7th, 14th, 21st, and 28th of January 2019 Gregorian approximately 7 days in between ironically all on a Monday. It doesn't always line up that way so kinda rare. It is simple actually the phase that falls closest to the 7 day interval is the sabbath 4 moons a month, new, first quarter, full, then last quarter Moon. Full Moon is 21st January, 7 days between mostly then 28th another Sabbath Day.  The phases several days so sometimes time for a feast depends on the season but the tribes all saw the Moon and it was their clock in the sky. A very simple system of telling time and setting up meetings on foot, or horseback, as no hurry then took days just to get anywhere, no trains to catch in those times. The Moon osculates but the average is maintained anyhow that is how the ancient tribesman calculated the Sabbath days for the rest periods. The new moon day can be calculated as neutral it seems sometimes. As I said time moved slow in those days no jets to catch so a few hours or a day to realign didn't matter as the Moon sufficed.

# Destruction of Jerusalem 70 AD

By Flavius Josephus
BOOK VI
CHAPTER 9.
What Injunctions Caesar Gave When He Was Come Within The
City. The Number Of The Captives And Of Those That Perished
In The Siege; As Also Concerning Those That Had Escaped Into
The Subterranean Caverns, Among Whom Were The Tyrants Simon
And John Themselves. Now when Titus was come into this [upper] city, he admired not only some other places of strength in it, but particularly those strong towers which the tyrants in their mad conduct had relinquished; for when he saw their solid altitude, and the largeness of their several stones, and the exactness of their joints, as also how great was their breadth, and how extensive their length, he expressed himself after the manner following: "We have certainly had God for our assistant in this war, and it was no other than God who ejected the Jews out of these fortifications; for what could the hands of men or any machines do towards overthrowing these towers?" At which time he had many such discourses to his friends; he also let such go free as had been bound by the tyrants, and were left in the prisons. To conclude, when he entirely demolished the rest of the city, and overthrew its walls, he left these towers as a monument of his good fortune, which had proved his auxiliaries, and enabled him to take what could not otherwise have been taken by him. And now, since his soldiers were already quite tired with killing men, and yet there appeared to be a vast multitude still remaining alive, Caesar gave orders that they should kill none but those that were in arms, and opposed them, but should take the rest alive. But, together with those whom they had orders to slay, they slew the aged and the infirm; but for those that were in their flourishing age, and who might be useful to them, they drove them together into the temple, and shut them up within the walls of the court of the women; over which Caesar set one of his freed-men, as also Fronto, one of his own friends; which last was to determine every one's fate, according to his merits. So this Fronto slew all those that had been seditious and robbers, who were impeached one by another; but of the young men he chose out the tallest and most beautiful, and reserved them for the triumph; and as for the rest of the multitude that were above seventeen years old, he put them into bonds, and sent them to the Egyptian mines.

Titus also sent a great number into the provinces, as a present to them, that they might be destroyed upon their theaters, by the sword and by the wild beasts; but those that were under seventeen years of age were sold for slaves. Now during the days wherein Fronto was distinguishing these men, there perished, for want of food, eleven thousand; some of whom did not taste any food, through the hatred their guards bore to them; and others would not take in any when it was given them. The multitude also was so very great, that they were in want even of corn for their sustenance. Now the number of those that were carried captive during this whole war was collected to be ninety-seven thousand; as was the number of those that perished during the whole siege eleven hundred thousand, the greater part of whom were indeed of the same nation [with the citizens of Jerusalem], but not belonging to the city itself; for they were come up from all the country to the feast of unleavened bread, and were on a sudden shut up by an army, which, at the very first, occasioned so great a straitness among them, that there came a pestilential destruction upon them, and soon afterward such a famine, as destroyed them more suddenly. And that this city could contain so many people in it, is manifest by that number of them which was taken under Cestius, who being desirous of informing Nero of the power of the city, who otherwise was disposed to contemn that nation, entreated the high priests, if the thing were possible, to take the number of their whole multitude. So these high priests, upon the coming of that feast which is called the Passover, when they slay their sacrifices, from the ninth hour till the eleventh, but so that a company not less than ten 33 belong to every sacrifice, [for it is not lawful for them to feast singly by themselves,] and many of us are twenty in a company, found the number of sacrifices was two hundred and fifty-six thousand five hundred; which, upon the allowance of no more than ten that feast together, amounts to two millions seven hundred thousand and two hundred persons that were pure and holy; for as to those that have the leprosy, or the gonorrhea, or women that have their monthly courses, or such as are otherwise polluted, it is not lawful for them to be partakers of this sacrifice; nor indeed for any foreigners neither, who come hither to worship. Now this vast multitude is indeed collected out of remote places, but the entire nation was now shut up by fate as in prison, and the Roman army encompassed the city when it was crowded with inhabitants. Accordingly, the multitude of those that therein perished exceeded all the destructions that either men or God ever brought upon the world; for, to speak only of what was publicly known, the Romans slew some of them, some they carried captives, and others they made a search for under ground, and when they found where they were, they broke up the ground and slew all they met with.

There were also found slain there above two thousand persons, partly by their own hands, and partly by one another, but chiefly destroyed by the famine; but then the ill savor of the dead bodies was most offensive to those that lighted upon them, insomuch that some were obliged to get away immediately, while others were so greedy of gain, that they would go in among the dead bodies that lay on heaps, and tread upon them; for a great deal of treasure was found in these caverns, and the hope of gain made every way of getting it to be esteemed lawful. Many also of those that had been put in prison by the tyrants were now brought out; for they did not leave off their barbarous cruelty at the very last: yet did God avenge himself upon them both, in a manner agreeable to justice.

As for John, he wanted food, together with his brethren, in these caverns, and begged that the Romans would now give him their right hand for his security, which he had often proudly rejected before; but for Simon, he struggled hard with the distress he was in, still he was forced to surrender himself, as we shall relate hereafter; so he was reserved for the triumph, and to be then slain; as was John condemned to perpetual imprisonment. And now the Romans set fire to the extreme parts of the city, and burnt them down, and entirely demolished its walls. Josephus (a personal witness to the events) claims that over 1,100,000 people were killed during the initial siege, of which a majority were Jewish. 97,000 were captured and enslaved, and many fled to areas around the Mediterranean. Titus reportedly refused to accept a wreath of victory, as there is "no merit in vanquishing people forsaken by their own God." During the siege, there was mass starvation in which cannibalism widely occurred with, it is believed, some mothers even devouring their own children. Later, there were even mass crucifixions to the degree that wood eventually became unavailable.  But the number of calamities which everywhere fell upon the nation at that time; the extreme misfortunes to which the inhabitants of Judea were especially subjected, the thousands of men, as well as women and children, that perished by the sword, by famine, and by other forms of death innumerable—all these things, as well as the many great sieges which were carried on against the cities of Judea, and the excessive sufferings endured by those that fled to Jerusalem itself, as to a city of perfect safety, and finally the general course of the whole war, as well as its particular occurrences in detail, and how at last the abomination of desolation, proclaimed by the prophets, Daniel 9:27 stood in the very temple of God, so celebrated of old, the temple which was now awaiting its total and final destruction by fire — all these things any one that wishes may find accurately described in the history written by Josephus.

### Matthew 24:21

" For then shall be great tribulation, such as was not since the beginning of the kingdom of Judea to this time, no, nor ever shall be.

## Crucifixion A Hoax

### John 19: 6 – 8

As soon as the chief priests and their officials saw him, they shouted,

"Crucify! Crucify!"

But Pilate answered,

"You take him and crucify him. As for me, I find no basis for a charge against him."

The Jewish leaders insisted,

"We have a law, and according to that law he must die, because he claimed to be the Son of Yahweh."
When Pilate heard this, he was even more afraid, and he went back inside the palace.

"Where do you come from?"

He asked Yahshua, but Yahshua gave him no answer.

"Do you refuse to speak to me?" Pilate said. "Don't you realize I have power either to free you or to crucify you?"

Okay notice Pilate openly states that he finds Yahshua innocent, and lets him know that he has the power to set him free, nevertheless the mob wanted him dead. So Pilate hatched a plan to save Yahshua. So a secret plan was set into motion.

**John 19: 28-30**

" Later, knowing that everything had now been finished, ( Secret plan was executed ) and so that Scripture would be fulfilled, Yahshua said,

"I am thirsty."

A jar of wine vinegar was there, so they soaked a sponge in it, put the sponge on a stalk of the hyssop plant, and lifted it to Yahshua's ' lips. When he had received the drink, Yahshua said,

"It is finished."

With that, he bowed his head and gave up his breath."

What actually happened here was Yahshua was drugged and knocked out with a very strong potion which almost immediately rendered him unconscious, according to the plan.

**John 19:38-40**

" Later, Joseph of Arimathea asked Pilate for the body of Yahshua. Now Joseph was a disciple of Yahshua , but secretly because he feared the Jewish leaders. With Pilate's permission, he came and took the body away. He was accompanied by Nicodemus, the man who earlier had visited Yahshua at night. Nicodemus brought a mixture of myrrh and aloes, about seventy-five pounds, Taking Yahshua' body, the two of them wrapped it, with the spices, in strips of linen."

Arimathea as well Nicodemus knew Yahshua was just unconscious, but they knew they had to act quickly because of the stab wound so they got Yahshua down very quickly and immediately began attending his wounds thus stopping the bleeding. Notice that Nicodemus had visited Yahshua earlier to go over the secret plan, all of course with Pilate's permission who was actually in on the plan from the beginning. Amazing to think that, " myrrh and aloes " were potions used on the living not the dead, in those days this medicine was called, Marham-i-Isa.

**Matthew 27:57-**

"As evening approached, there came a rich man from Arimathea, named Joseph, who had himself become a disciple of Yahshua . Going to Pilate, he asked for Yahshua's body, and Pilate ordered that it be given to him. Joseph took the body, wrapped it in a clean linen cloth, and placed it in his own new tomb that he had cut out of the rock. He rolled a big stone in front of the entrance to the tomb and went away."

This is a brand new tomb still under construction, so there was more than one entry point still unsealed, a back door. Also noticed as evening approached so it was still very light out, but Arimathea was wasting no time getting this unconscious body into this new tomb, with life saving medicine including the antidote. Also notice that Nicodemus did not leave with the Arimathean but still was left inside the tomb with Yahshua as a nurse.

**Matthew 27: 62-66**

" The next day, the one after Preparation Day, the chief priests and the Pharisees went to Pilate."Sir," they said, "we remember that while he was still alive that deceiver said, 'After three days I will rise again.' So give the order for the tomb to be made secure until the third day. Otherwise, his disciples may come and steal the body and tell the people that he has been raised from the dead. This last deception will be worse than the first." "Take a guard," Pilate answered. "Go, make the tomb as secure as you know how." So they went and made the tomb secure by putting a seal on the stone and posting the guard.

**Matthew 28:11-15**

" While the women were on their way, some of the guards went into the city and reported to the chief priests everything that had happened. When the chief priests had met with the elders and devised a plan, they gave the soldiers a large sum of money, telling them, "You are to say, 'His disciples came during the night and stole him away while we were asleep.' If this report gets to the governor, we will satisfy him and keep you out of trouble." So the soldiers took the money and did as they were instructed. And this story has been widely circulated among the Jews to this very day."

## John 20: 1-2

"Early on the first day of the week, while it was still dark, Mary Magdalene went to the tomb and saw that the stone had been removed from the entrance. So she came running to Simon Peter and the other disciple, the one Yahshua loved, and said, "They have taken the Lord out of the tomb, and we don't know where they have put him!"

Of course no body was found, because Yahshua was revived as planned , and was hanging out about the place but with a disguise.

## John 20: 19-22

" On the evening of that first day of the week, when the disciples were together, with the doors locked for fear of the Jewish leaders, Yahshua came and stood among them and said, "Peace be with you!" After he said this, he showed them his hands and side. The disciples were overjoyed when they saw the Lord. Again Yahshua said, "Peace be with you! As the Father has sent me, I am sending you." And with that he breathed on them and said, "Receive the Sacred Breath"

According to this Yahshua had survived the ordeal quite well as the wounds were already healing, which is the main evidence that this was the physical Yahshua in the flesh and blood, but the biggest clue is when he breaths on them showing that he was truly alive and not dead.
Yes, the so called, Crucifixion of " Jesus Christ " is one of the greatest hoax ever perpetrated on mankind. When in fact Yahshua didn't die on the cross but lived on. Of course he had to get the heck out of Jerusalem so he did.

## Acts 1: 3-9

" After his suffering, he presented himself to them and gave many convincing proofs that he was alive. He appeared to them over a period of forty days and spoke about the kingdom of Elohim. On one occasion, while he was eating with them, he gave them this command:
"Do not leave Jerusalem, but wait for the gift my Father promised, ( The Promised Land ) which you have heard me speak about. For John baptized with water, but in a few days you will be baptized with the Sacred Breath ."

Then they gathered around him and asked him, "Lord, are you at this time going to restore the kingdom to Israel?" He said to them: "It is not for you to know the times or dates the Father has set by his own authority. But you will receive power when the Sacred Breath comes on you; and you will be my witnesses in Jerusalem, and in all Judea and Samaria, and to the ends of the earth."
After he said this, he was taken up before their very eyes, and a cloud hid him from their sight."

Okay so Yahshua hung out about the place forty days convincing his followers he was truly alive and the whole dying on the cross was a myth. Yahshua however knew he had to go make ready for the escape of the 144,000 once gathered from the tribes so he went up into the mountains just below the cloud level to say farewell then simply stepped back up the mountain a bit and vanished into the clouds. They asked, Yahshua about the restoration of the Kingdom of Israel, but as wisely stated he didn't even know at that time if such a place could be found, " and to the ends of the earth " means we are going to find a place if we have to search the whole planet.

"Men of Galilee," they said, "why do you stand here looking into the sky? This same Yahshua , who has been taken from you into heaven,( The place or state of existence of the blessed, ie- Healthy Atmosphere) will come back in the same way you have seen him go into heaven."

**Matthew 10: 23**

" When they persecute you in one town, flee to the next. Truly I tell you, you will not reach all the towns of Israel before the Son of Man comes."

Again, as stated the news of the gathering away was happening quickly for the time was short, in fact gathering up 144,000 people from the twelve tribes of Israel to leave every thing and travel far away into unknown territory would be quite a task, but with the leadership of such a wise teacher as Yahshua it did happen successfully.

**Revelation 12: 5-7**

" And she gave birth to a son, a male child, who will rule all the tribes with an iron scepter; and her child was caught up to Elohim and to His throne. The woman fled into the wilderness, where Yahweh had prepared a place for her to be nourished for one thousand two hundred sixty days. Then a war broke out in heaven: Michael and his messengers fought against the dragon, and the dragon and his messengers fought back. …"

So Yahshua went into the wilderness with other elders to scout out a path for the 144,000 Israelite to follow during the escape from Judea that was quickly to come about, for tensions between the Romans and Israelite were already brewing. They knew there had to be provisions, and as well a stealthy path north that would not be easily detected. The one thousand two hundred sixty days is just simply the time it will take on the journey as calculations, and hookup dates were set. Of course by this time the War with Rome had already begun.

**John 14: 2-4**

" In My Father's house are many pastures. If it were not so, would I have told you that I am going there to prepare a place for you? And if I go and prepare a place for you, I will come back and welcome you into My presence, so that you also may be where I am. You know the way to the place where I am going."…

Speaking of the 144,000 that are to be made ready for the journey.
The Father's house is simply the House of Israel, the nation including all twelve tribes. The place is a new land somewhere, even Yahshua didn't know exactly the times or the place so they set out exploring for a place they could live free from the Romans as well the Rule of evil Kings like Herod, but they did have the promise that Yahshua would return for them once such a place was found.

" To the ends of the earth! "

# The 144,000

Rome's destruction of Jerusalem began in 66 AD, when Roman Emperor Nero appointed General Titus Flavius Vespasianus to put down a revolt in Judea.

**Luke 21: 19-21**

"By your patient endurance, you will gain your souls. But when you see Jerusalem surrounded by armies, you will know that her desolation is near. Then let those in Judea flee to the mountains, let those in the city get out, and let those in the country stay out of the city."

Yahshua and his followers knew the Roman Armies were going to come against Judea at Jerusalem so he tipped his people off with this coded message embedded in a message. A warning that once the siege begins the city will be surrounded quickly barring any escape so they knew to get out, leave then head for the gathering place as previously planned ahead of time. In those days messengers were runners that physically carried the letter between groups. Some of these carriers would get captured by the Romans so the message had to be coded in such a way that would seem a bit of nonsense.

**Matthew 24:14-16**

" And this gospel of the kingdom( 144,000) will be preached in all of Judea as a testimony to all tribes , and then the end will come. So when you see standing in the holy place 'the abomination of desolation,' described by the prophet Daniel (let the reader understand), then let those in Judea flee to the mountains. Let no one on the housetop come down to retrieve anything from his house. And let no one in the field return for his cloak. How miserable those days will be for pregnant and nursing mothers!
"

This text is written in similar fashion, but as it states the news will not be spread about the many tribes before the Roman Armies would come bringing the end to the age of Judea. But again a warning to the tribes of Israel to be prepared to leave at the drop of a hat when the armies of Rome begin to appear. You can get a sense of how serious the urgency of this matter will be as one could imagine a young mother attempting to flea the Roman Army with a young child.

## Matthew 10: 23

"When they persecute you in one town, flee to the next. Truly I tell you, you will not reach all the towns of Israel before the Son of Man comes."

Again, as stated the news of the gathering away was happening quickly for the time was short, in fact,

## Matthew 24:22

" If those days had not been cut short, nobody would be saved."

Even the 144,000 would of been killed, or become Roman slaves  But for the sake of the elect,( 144,000 ) those days will be shortened. In other words they got out left ahead of schedule.

## Matthew 16: 28

"Truly I tell you, some who are standing here will not taste death until they see the Son of Man coming in His kingdom."

The messiah, Yahshua was collecting up citizens for the new kingdom gathering of the New Jerusalem, that will escape the Roman army, for the old kingdom was coming to an end, so in fact true enough most of the people that accepted the plea to leave where of the younger generation less indoctrinated as the text states where young as would be awhile before death implying not that old yet, of course those that stayed or didn't believe the message met a different fate.

## Revelations 7: 1-8

"After this I saw four messengers standing at the four corners of the earth, holding back the four winds of the earth to prevent any wind from blowing on the land or on the sea or on any tree. Then I saw another messenger coming up from the east, having the seal of the living Elohim . He called out in a loud voice to the four messengers who had been given power to harm the land and the sea: "Do not harm the land or the sea or the trees until we put a seal on the foreheads of the servants of our Elohim."

Then I heard the number of those who were sealed: 144,000 from all the tribes of Israel. From the tribe of Judah 12,000 were sealed, from the tribe of Reuben 12,000, from the tribe of Gad 12,000, from the tribe of Asher 12,000, from the tribe of Naphtali 12,000, from the tribe of Manasseh 12,000, from the tribe of Simeon 12,000, from the tribe of Levi 12,000, from the tribe of Issachar 12,000, from the tribe of Zebulun 12,000, from the tribe of Joseph 12,000, from the tribe of Benjamin 12,000."

This is nothing more than the manifest of the numbers of people to make ready for the long journey north fleeing over the mountains into Europe far away from the Roman Armies towards a new beginning, a new age. The Exodus from Jerusalem with Yahshua and other elders leading them sometime around the year 66 A.D.

**Revelation 14:1-2**

" Then I looked and saw the Lamb standing on Mount Zion, and with Him one hundred forty-four thousand who had His name and His Father's name written on their foreheads. And I heard a sound from heaven like the roar of rushing waters and the loud rumbling of thunder. And the sound I heard was like harpists strumming their harps...."

This is a statement of the fact that Yahshua did escape the Roman Armies with the 144,000 children of Israel with tickets in hand metaphorically for the trip sealed, while at the same time the sounds of the War could already be heard from the valleys below as the Roman Army unleashes on Jerusalem

**Revelation 14:3-5**

" And they sang a new song before the throne and before the four living creatures and the elders. And no one could learn the song except the 144,000 who had been redeemed from Israel. These are the ones who have not been defiled with women, for they are pure. They follow the Lamb wherever He goes. They have been redeemed from among men as first fruits to Yahweh and to the Lamb. And no lie was found in their mouths; they are blameless."

Children, the 144,000 were children, probably most younger than twenty one. Think about it as you listen to the text here, who has not been with a woman? Children. As it actually states pure. So these were 12,000 children, and young adults mostly gathered up from among each twelve tribes of Israel able bodied, ready to make the flight north into Europe evading the Roman Armies. As children do we are sure they were making up new songs as they were sprinting along. These very children made that journey as are now current day part of the many European nations and as promised also many of their decedents migrated further to a new world in America.

## Mark OF The Beast

First Century A.D.

We have always suspected that the mark of the beast was the Caesar's minted coins as the whole Render unto Caesar, bit was actually about giving all the money back to Rome not even using their currency. In other words not accepting the Mark of Caesar at all. The remaining Jews we are sure after the lose of Judea some quite appalled at being forced to trade only with Caesar coin then later Emperor Constantine making it law throughout the whole empire must trade in Roman Marks, as well accept the new Christianize Mithra religion or die.. Yah, We agree all past tense, what a shame how so many people are fooled into thinking this is still yet future.

This message prompted more research into this very famous subject and this is what have found so far. Okay we will take some of the scriptures referencing to the, Mark of the Beast and detail our thoughts on the subject while projecting our minds into that time period and observing objectively.

**Revelation Chapter 13: 16-**

" -And he causeth all, both small and great, rich and poor, free and bond, to receive a mark in their right hand, or in their foreheads: And that no man might buy or sell, save he that had the mark, or the name of the beast, or the number of his name. Here is wisdom. Let him that hath understanding count the number of the beast: for it is the number of a man; and his number [is] Six hundred threescore [and] six. "

Okay after Judea fell to Titus of Rome, many Israelites were taken as slaves and stripped of their previous titles, estates, as it says rich, or poor, free or bond, all were branded both on the right hand, or on their foreheads to distinguish them from Roman citizens, which was common practice for the Roman army. The Beast simply means Emperor of Rome which in this case is Nero. The number 666 (DCLXVI) is simply the date year 66, 6th month, Nero (first beast) as well 666 also may have been used on the marks either tattoos or coins as the date officially the Jews were deemed full property as slaves of the Roman Empire. ( Similar like how 911 is used today after a tragedy - marker in time for Bin Laden ) All this took place between 66 and the fall of Judea along with the destruction of the temple, 70 AD all past tense.

**Revelation 14: 9 – 14**

" - And the third messenger followed them, saying with a loud voice, If any man worship the beast and his image, and receive [his] mark in his forehead, or in his hand, The same shall drink of the wine of the wrath of Yahweh, which is poured out without mixture into the cup of his indignation; and he shall be tormented with fire and brimstone in the presence of the sacred messengers, and in the presence of the Lamb: And the smoke of their torment ascendeth up for ever and ever: and they have no rest day nor night, who worship the beast and his image, and whosoever receiveth the mark of his name. "

Okay, this is somewhat different language but its interpretation is simple. If any man worship the beast implies volunteer, convert without force basically joining the Roman Mithra Catholic religion, instead of holding fast to the way of life set forth by Yahshua remaining, Yahwist - which in those days if caught practicing this lifestyle within the Roman Empire meant death, at the hands of the Roman Rulers or in the Roman Colosseum. So those who turn their back on what they understand as truth and accept the false religions just to save their own skins will not fair well with Karma.. Angel simply means, Messenger, the one who is writing this message, a Apostle, or disciple of Yahshua the Messiah, taking notes, a reporter, the press.

**Revelation 20:4**

" - And I saw thrones, and they sat upon them, and judgment was given unto them: and [I saw] the souls of them that were beheaded for the witness of Yahshua, and for the word of Yahweh, and which had not worshiped the beast, neither his image, neither had received [his] mark upon their foreheads, or in their hands; and they lived and reigned with messiah a thousand years. "

Okay the souls of them that were beheaded for the witness of Yahshua are those that were killed by the Romans in the Colosseum, or otherwise that knew Yahshua, maybe a Apostle, or disciple, or follower that would not join or accept the Emperor's false pagan religion. Also notice, " and for the word of Yahweh " See every scrap of scripture scroll, or book was being burned or confiscated. Why do you think the Dead Sea Scrolls were so hidden in caves? Same reason the Yahshua movement was to be completely squished out.

This was serious stuff in the first century and centuries to follow, as false so called Christian religion was being forced upon the people instead. Of course all the rage is only trying to get your attention as to how serious this is, in fact so much time, money and energy is absorbed into these false rituals they could actually destroy our planet if left unchecked.

" - and they lived and reigned with their Messiah a thousand years. "

Basically means they knew, followed, and believed Yahshua as their teacher as they will not be forgotten but remembered by future generations to come as we still read about these thousands of years later, but because of their sacrifice the movement survived. By the way, " Christ " simply means savior or messiah, i.e. Someone who leads his people to safety during war times. This also is fulfilled as Yahshua did in fact lead 144,000 Hebrew Israelite from 12 tribes out of Judea thus surviving the whole ordeal with the Roman Armies thus a true Savior of his times. Yahshua was not crucified as the false religion would have you to believe, but instead as it is stated, lived and reigned.

## Revelation 4:7

" -And the first beast was like a lion, and the second beast like a calf, and the third beast had a face as a man, and the fourth beast was like a flying eagle."

All Roman Emperor Dynasties four in All after the invention of Mithran Catholicism leading up to Emperor Constantine that finalized the false religion as the official State Religion of the Great Roman Empire and went forth killing and conquering millions then the minds of billions in the name of Jesus the Antichrist ( The personified LORD GOD Emperor ) with the Holy Cross image as its Catholic symbol. Basically the symbol of the sword with a mutilated, cleaved, punctured unconscious man hanging off it.

## Revelation 19: 20

" - And the beast was taken, and with him the false prophet that wrought miracles before him, with which he deceived them that had received the mark of the beast, and them that worshiped his image. These both were cast alive into a lake of fire burning with brimstone."

Basically this is saying the deception will end someday, first the Roman Military Might under the Emperors which has basically already happened with the fall of the Roman Empire ( In 476 C.E. Romulus, the last of the Roman emperors in the west, was overthrown. Then more recently the fall of the British Empire which was basically a mirror image of the Roman Empire just under the Church of England instead. As of now what of the mighty Catholic Church, the Vatican and the false religions, the Antichrist and the final Beast, " The Pope " ?  The one that still has this illusion over a billion followers under the False Prophet ( False Jesus Anti-Christ ) the one that brought so many miracles which has deceived so many human beings upon this planet. --- Those who worship His Image On the Cross crucified but whose deadly wound was healed resurrected from the dead as a GOD born from the Virgin Mary.

## Revelation 13:3

" - I saw that one of the heads of the beast seemed wounded beyond recovery--but the fatal wound was healed! The whole world marveled at this miracle and gave allegiance to the beast. "

Notice it says, " Whole World" Well seems both the Empires and the False Religions will end soon in a fire. This fire is the light of the truth as human beings all over this planet wake up into this dawn of this brand new age of enlightenment, a true age of truth and light energy for all.

Pope's Fisherman's ring will be destroyed using a special silver hammer. The moment symbolizes the end of the Pope's authority and also serves a more practical purpose. It is a signet ring, used to officially seal documents and ensure their authenticity as,

" The Mark of the Beast "
Constantine Sees a Vision of the Cross

**Matthew 10:34**

" - But whoever denies Me before men, I will also deny him before My Father in heaven. Do not assume that I have come to bring peace to the earth; I have not come to bring peace, but a sword. For I have come to turn 'A man against his father, a daughter against her mother, a daughter-in-law against her mother-in-law. "

Why do people call Jesus Christ the prince of peace when in fact according to this passage he is the opposite. Of course this isn't Yahshua speaking here. This is the Emperor pretending to be God's Son and talking to his Father in his Holy Church he is building for the Empire. Basically what he is saying is oppose me, or our new religion you will die. Forget family, family is useless for Rome you must join the legions and learn how to wheel a sword. No time to settle down and raise a family, you must become Nuns and Priest for our great cause for our new Great Catholic Religion. So a contradiction or was it?

Of course Yahshua was teaching love your Neighbor as yourself. Neighbors live in neighborhoods full of families, and family farms within a community, or kingdom. In nature we still refer to nature as kingdoms as the Plants, Animals, Protists, Fungi, Archaebacteria and Eubacteria Kingdoms.

## Mark 12: 15-

" - Teacher," they said, "we know that You are honest and are swayed by no one. Indeed, You are impartial and teach the way of Yahweh in accordance with the truth. Now then, is it lawful to pay taxes to Caesar or not? Should we pay them or not?" But Yahshua saw through their hypocrisy and said, "Why are you testing Me? Bring Me a denarius to inspect." So they brought it, and He asked them, "Whose likeness is this? And whose inscription?" "Caesar's," they answered. Then Yahshua told them, "Give to Caesar what is Caesar's, and to Yahweh what is Yahweh's." And they marveled at Him.…."

Okay how do you know if something belongs to someone? The coin belongs to Caesar because Caesar has put his signature upon it as his. So give him his coin. If it were your coin it would have your inscription on it, right so give the coin back to Caesar. End of story but what else did Yahshua say here?

Give to Yahweh what is Yahweh's WOW! How do we humans give the creator being what belongs to the creator. The creator being is spirit and lives inside us all, no image, no idol, no form, just pure creative energy.. Ask yourself what can you give my life's energy to? A factory building swords for Caesar maybe, or working to restore this Planet Eden a much better place for our children, or simply helping someone in need, or as Yahshua was doing being a teacher for the Good News, a brotherhood of man within this wonderful Kingdom of Heaven.

## Revelation 11:18

"-The nations were angry, and your wrath has come. The time has come for judging the dead, and for rewarding your servants the prophets and your people who revere your name, both great and small-- and for destroying those who destroy the earth."

Angry nations sound familiar? Your wrath has come simply means the wrath of nature, super storms, volcanoes, mega earthquakes, tsunami, floods, fires, yes many will not survive, basically upheaval in the earth. But what look here at this distinction,

" Your people who revere your name "

People that live simple lives, loving, caring with nature, community, family, folks trying to save what is left of Eden the great garden of Elohim. Folks that kept and stuck with Yahshua's teachings all down through genetic time. But look what is next ~

" and for destroying those who destroy the earth. "

The final act then finally, Peace On Earth for All. We are nearing the end of the time, times and half a time, the two thousand, and five hundred years allowed for the Beasts to roam and destroy this earth spoken of by the prophet Daniel.

Rome becomes a republic in 509 B.C - The Ottoman Turks capture Constantinople in 1453 A.D - The transfer of Hong Kong to China in 1997 marked the end of the British Empire - Catholics in the United States dropped by 3 million since 2007 Catholicism loses more members than it gains at a higher rate than any other denomination, with nearly 13 percent of all Americans describing themselves as "former Catholics. The marker in time is achieved we are within a new age of mankind, a new dispensation, and it is obvious everywhere real time here and now.

" The abomination of desolation shall end ! "

We live in a time now when all these things are coming to pass all around us all the time but we don't have to lift up a sword against anybody, just shine your light out over this dark world, and illuminate the good still left alive within our beloved planet and her beloved people, then let nature do the rest. She knows, Gaia comes in her season, and her season is now, her time has come, the signs are everywhere, yet her spirit breaths, hovering over the waters ushering us all back into the fold.

**Isaiah 2:4**

" - Yahweh Elohim will mediate between nations and will settle international disputes. They will hammer their swords into plowshares and their spears into pruning hooks. Nation will no longer fight against nation, nor train for war anymore. "

Still yet future we cannot date when this scripture may happen but we believe soon. We are not there yet so there is still a lot of work to be done on this Earth yet. What we do know is that when this does happen a lot of money, and energy, and lives will be redirected, that now are going into the war machines. Forced funding duplicated within every nation on earth training for war, that could go into feeding the hungry, or housing the homeless, or healing the sick, or just inventing something better, more useful, more practical than killing each other.

## Ancient Books And Fake News

The bible was designed to contradict itself. Why do you think this book has caused so much division in the world? It is total madness every time someone revises, or translates this thing they have always added in their own pet doctrines from Emperor Constantine to King James, to Billy Graham, to the point our modern versions are so different from the originals there simply is no comparison. Now even with all the hocus pocus mumbo jumbo one can still find some kernels of truth. General rule of thumb if it seems far fetched and unnatural it is more than likely a fable, myth, or total crap added in by some church, religion, or cult. ( For instance human virgins giving birth to Gods, Or resurrections from the dead, or forgiveness of sins when every action has equal and opposite reaction as you sow you reap karma. ) Humans may forgive each other but the Universe probably will not because there are underlying physical laws at work here on the quantum level. Do some research, study learn to love the quest for truth. You will find that at the end of the day one must put away the books and just simply go out into the forest, or a garden or beside a river somewhere, be quiet and listen cause the Elohim of Eden is still here all around us all the time whispering the wisdom of the ages. If any of the parents, ( Our Fathers in Heaven ) all down from our ancestry would not of survived till childbearing years, you wouldn't be here today. ( We still call this the family tree, or bloodline.) We all come from parents for millions of years handing down their DNA to us living today so in a way we all have been living forever. The same is true for the future so pass it along, " Life is eternal unless we kill our planet because extinction also is forever. Such a fine line we walk out into the cosmos. The tribes of Men knew this knowledge, some few hundred years ago in the Americas. False religions took it all away from them with money cults and Kings mad for gold, and armies of death, greed and debt.

These same evil cults took it from the actual tribes of Israel some 2000 years ago. Now imagine that! Whats Next? Extinction Total! Unless Natural Human Beings upon this planet wake up and begin to speak the ancient knowledge stored within them eternally!~

For Instance,

**Matthew 6:9-**

"Our Father in heaven, hallowed be your name. ( Honor your father and your mother so that your days may be long upon the earth ) Your kingdom come, your will be done, on earth as it is in heaven.( Our children's children's childrens' live long healthy lives without war or disease) Give us this day our daily bread, ( Healthy Food without poison yet organic nourishment) and forgive us our debts, as we also have forgiven our debtors. ( No interest, no loans, no debt, no tithes, no taxes) And lead us not into temptation, ( Give us sound minds that will not waver from truth forever ) but deliver us from evil.'" The war machine, the atomic power, the false religions, the false gods, the artificial worlds, mega cities, the idolatrous nations of greed, pollution, disease, deceit, and unnatural death. There are thousands of mistranslations in the bible. Boy, this really opens up a can of worms maybe the Catholic Church will begin to tell the rest. " Fall" really? Temptation is within the mind of man there is no leading or falling involved it begins with a thought that can, " lead " to action so there is a decision to be made within the consciousness of a human being. In Roman times of course the " Father in heaven " referred to the Sun as they were Sun Worshipers. " --and with every wicked deception directed against those who are perishing, because they refused the love of the truth that would have saved them. For this reason, GOD will send them a powerful delusion so that they will," believe " the lie, in order that judgment will come upon all who have disbelieved the truth and delighted in wickedness. "

**2 Thessalonians 2:10-11 also Matthew 23:9**

" And do not call anyone on earth 'father,' for you have one Father, and he is in heaven."

So who are all these false so called, " Fathers " within this Catholic Church people ( Believers ) are confessing to? Yes, the delusion is revealed. Notice who is sending this " powerful delusion " none other than the God Almighty. Now ask yourself, " What is this truth that saves us? "

Remember the Garden of Eden, the tree of life, the one that if humans eat from they live forever on earth with their children for thousands of generations, yes the lovers and keepers of nature's truth. " Our Daily Bread. ( BTW- This world should forgive all debts in fact all debts should be forgiven globally immediately, especially national debts everywhere, a international year of jubilee could actually save this planet. Why pray a prayer if people are not willing to make it come true? )

In addition to these Hebrew-speaking settlements in Judea, the priests in the Temple were for the most part still speaking Hebrew, and Hebrew remained a language of the law spoken and studied by the rabbis. But this was only the upper class of Judean society. Most people couldn't read in any language. Modern scholarship estimates that the literacy rate in Roman Palestine was 3 percent and probably much lower in a rural backwater town like Nazareth. Hebrew died off as a spoken language by the end of the century, but continued to remain an important religious language for the Jews, though later religious texts most notably the Talmud would be written in Aramaic. ( Thinking he was in their company, they traveled on for a day. Then they began looking for him among their relatives and friends. When they did not find him, they went back to Yahrusalem to look for him. After three days they found him in the temple courts, sitting among the teachers, listening to them and asking them questions. )

So Yahshua as 12 years was learning the language spoken in the Temple and that language was Hebrew.

**Matthew 24:15 ---**

" So when you see standing in the holy place 'the abomination of desolation,' ( Roman Armies under Nero year 66-6 AD) described by the prophet Daniel (let the reader understand), then let those in Judea flee to the mountains. Let no one on the housetop come down to retrieve anything from his house. "

( 144,000 from the tribes fled light footed without heavy belongings)---- Flavius Josephus, The Wars of the Jews. ( Why do you think they were up on their housetops? They were watching for the Roman Armies.) Regardless of what one may find in some books nevertheless Yahweh, ( Invisible spirit creator without image or form ) has been replaced by the Trinity GOD Head, ( A Idol with form, a image) among most Christian church cults with Jesus Christ worshiped as a GOD.

All proper names are transliterated not translated when transferring between languages so seems the Scribes did a lot of deliberate tampering with early scraps of new testament scripture ( Mostly coded notes and letters being passed among the Jews during the seize of Jerusalem 1st century ) at the Council of Nicea 3rd century. (" LORD" - an appellation for a person or deity who has authority, control, or power over others acting like a master, a chief, or a ruler---- sounds more like the Emperor of Rome, Or a title for an English KING. ) Yet it seems that the actual story of Hebrew Yahshua the Savior of the Judeans in the first century by evading the Roman Armies, and the later invented story of Jesus Christ by the Council of Nicea for the Emperor of Rome, is as different as night and day. Yahweh was replaced with Jesus Christ ( LORD Hail Zeus Chrisna ) a Roman idea to unite the many religions within their empire, after Nero yet a personification in a book some call a Holy Bible. ( By the way, Emperor Nero thought of himself a God born from a Virgin Mother sound familiar? )

All these concepts were total nonsense to the Hebrews in Yahshua's time. ( Dead Sea Scrolls are written in Hebrew also ) What is amazing is how many people on this planet will accept this as truth without doing any research at all.

Creator Elohim planted in the original garden a tree of knowledge of good and evil. Every man or woman alive today still must choose wither to eat from this tree or not. The tree of life is also still there full of fruit uneaten, seems a lot of evil mixed with some good has been chosen more often as the two faced GOD still rules the conscience of humanity as Eden is still being turned into a wasteland for miners both past and future. What actually happened to the original Garden of Eden? It was mined probably strip mined and turned into a quarry. A metaphorical garden a tree of knowledge of good and evil. So Adam and Eve ( male & female) are not only tempted they acted on their temptations such is still the case with most men and women of these false artificial worlds we build Metropolitan Cities ( Babylon ) instead of learning to live with nature. Nature is still being destroyed at a very alarming rate. Some creatures may call that " EVIL" as extinction looms on the horizon. (Genesis 4:17 Cain made love to his wife, and she became pregnant and gave birth to Enoch. Cain was then building a city, and he named it after his son Enoch.-- Zillah also bore Tubal-cain; he was the forger of all instruments of bronze and iron.

## Genesis 2:12

" The gold of that land is exceptionally pure; aromatic resin and onyx stone are also found there."

Seems Adam's Sons quickly became city builders and miners instead of gardeners and shepherds. So much for tending and watching over the Garden of Eden, thus protecting the Tree of Life as commanded in Genesis 2:15-"

We are at a crossroads again in time as mega cities now cover over most of the once natural fertile lands, where if we do not begin to tend and watch over this great natural garden we all now call the, Mother Earth including putting away some of these foolish empty useless rituals within these false religions with billions of members, like for instance, Christmas that generates more trash and waste than any other fake holiday. Nevertheless otherwise as decreased foliage, urban thermo-mass, and greenhouse gasses cause earth to expand and heat up rapidly do expect extreme weather of all kinds from floods, to fires, to massive hurricanes, earthquakes, and tsunamis, you name it as nature, gone mad is basically Her, Mother Nature's way of cooling things back down while bringing about the woe to all mankind.. The human beings living on this planet didn't learn that lesson before as they all got way to busy eating from the wrong tree until the flood came and took them all away except a few such a bottle neck. I feel that this time we might not be so lucky, yet -

" With my soul have I desired Thee in the night; yea, with my spirit within me will I seek Thee early; for when Thy judgments are in the earth, the inhabitants of the world will learn righteousness. "

Janus the Roman Two Faced God

Some estimates over 33,000 different denominations, divisions within the divisive Christians, not to mention the other two false religions of the book that can not get along on a single planet ? Just building all these separate churches in all these cities is becoming a huge environmental problem not to mention the distractions otherwise, 1st, 2nd, 3rd, 4th, Baptist Church and ripping up more forest for another just to mention one. We have 32,999 more to go down the broad way that leads to destruction that the many have found. The multitudes, and multitudes in the valley of decision.

So there is becoming overwhelming evidence that Our Good News ( The Gospel ) has been tampered with in a very deliberate fashion by design to include many false beliefs systems that were practiced by the Romans and later incorporated as the Roman Catholic Church a state religion orchestrated by Emperor Constantine a known Mithra worshiper that desired to retain his religion in secret by implanting it strategically within the translated early versions of the Holy Bible. You would think that the Catholic Church would just come out and admit to all these fallacies, but don't expect that anytime soon, this has been their cash cow for way to long now.

The illusion is so strong, that those that know within the ranks are betting few people will ever actually take the time to study enough to get to the truth of this matter. People really need to learn how these false teachings got into their bibles, or else they could be destined to wander the halls of ignorance within the dark corridors of deception their whole lives. Nevertheless, nothing is hidden that will not be made manifest, nor is anything secret that will not be known and come to light. " ---- Akashic Records 101

" Enter through the narrow gate. For wide is the gate and broad is the way that leads to destruction, and many enter through it. But small is the gate and narrow the way that leads to life, and only a few find it."

## Earthling Hominoidea Sapien Solhumatan Terrarius

Still finding it amazing just how quickly the cults of man, cast then draw into the nets their slave fish.. A human baby hasn't hardly been in this world a minute before the cult system begins to set it hooks onto that human spirit. From birth certificates, to learning the alphabet of a particular human nationality. Almost immediately the human infant becomes indoctrinated, within some religious culture, the technology of the times, a preschool kiddie garden, a governmental system.. All passing fancies within the evolution of human kind into the many futures, and to think we as a species are just now beginning to explore alternatives to these age old entrapment.

"Come follow after Me, and I will make you fishers of men."

Now who wants to be caught like a fish in the net of some false religion, some fake god worship cult?

Of course the superimposed Jesus Christ is a fake, a hoax, a total invention from the collective imagination of Roman Imperialism. Some would go as far as to say that Jesus Christ is the personification of the Roman Emperors starting with Nero, a God King born from a virgin mother resurrected as the SUN GOD born on December 25th. (Mithraism 101) Nevertheless all that other stuff is also a fake, a hoax, a invention.. See the mind of man is very imaginative, the same minds like George Lucas was alive and well thousands of years ago, writing science fiction, myths, and fables like it was going out of style. The bit about the aliens, gods or angels having sex with human females all rubbish..  The children of Adam were the first Caucasians on planet earth forged from the ice age (12,000 B.C. ) when receded they migrated south to find other tribes of man of all the other older races .. The Adamites (Cro-magnon ) called themselves the Sons Of Yahweh and they did take wives from the other races of man, not Aliens, not Angels just Anglo Saxon- Period end of story the great isolation ended. To this day you breed a thoroughbred Caucasian with a full blooded Mongolian you still may get a giant.
Yes, pure evolution as all the fishers of men will be unemployed soon as nobody on this planet will ever take that artificial bait again, as this new era of self-sufficient human evolution has truly arrived and will sweep this planet like a storm. If your trust is in the Money God then yes you are a disciple for the money, nothing spiritual there just a circus monkey doing the trick it has been taught from birth. But go further to imagine the same emotional ignorant people have financed all the wars by donating not only their money, but their young men & women. Wrong! Nah nothing wrong it is the right thing to do support the lie in every way you can.. such ingrained is the brainwashing that it is in your DNA and might take 50 generations to breed that crap out of them. There has only been two Gods on this planet and they both have come in many forms, one is nature and the other is money.. But each human being still as always must choose which one to serve. To study nature in a scientific fashion for the betterment of all mankind, as well animal, and plant kind is very noble and godlike and has many rewards, but on the other hand to study money, the tax system , the banking system, commerce, trading, stocks, and such also can have many rewards as we now have mega cities that cover the planet like a death star machine that is killing the very nature we all depend on for life, so yes which God will win this cosmic battle.

We say Nature.. Satan is just another name for Man - Satan is Man, Man is Satan same creature, same spirit -- That is why Man must cast out Himself ( Satan ) to evolve into a higher life form. Of course the God of this world is Man, Look around you at all the mega cities of Man that cover this planet like a cancer.

Look into the skies of this world and see all the flying machines made by Man. But remember there is another GOD in this Earth the natural Earth not the world the Natural Planet and that GOD we modern humans have called, Nature ( Gaia) Man has the power to Kill Nature until Nature Kills the Man. That is the only Battle in heaven.

That is the only war on earth and that is the war on nature. Man is just now beginning to evolve into a creature that can live truly in harmony with the natural kingdoms that surround him the first true Earthling Hominoidea Sapien Solhumatan Terrarius.
The Ehsst

## Enochville of Nodium

### Genesis 4 ( 1200 BC IRON AGE)

Adam in Hebrew means - Pale skinned with red blushed face.
The Children of Adam--- After they left the isolated areas trapped by the ice during the last great ice age which has changed them in appearance with many new skills adapted for survival but as the ice melts massive glaciers retreat worldwide as they are once again reunited with the other tribes of the lands as the first Caucasians forged by ice a new race of man appears.

" So Cain went out from the Lord's ( Adam's) presence and lived in the land of Nod, east of Eden. Cain made love to his wife. and she became pregnant and gave birth to Enoch. Cain was then building a city, and he named it after his son Enoch. To Enoch was born Irad, and Irad was the father of Mehujael, and Mehujael was the father of Methushael, and Methushael was the father of Lamech. Lamech married two women, one named Adah and the other Zillah."

---Okay, notice the new skills of the new city builders as founding fathers a term still used today---

" Adah gave birth to Jabal; he was the father of those who live in tents and raise livestock.
(Milk drinking herdsmen, cowboys- not hunter-gatherer )

His brother's name was Jubal; he was the father of all who play stringed instruments and pipes.
(Craftsmen, musicians, artist, not stone tool makers)
Zillah also had a son, Tubal-Cain, who forged all kinds of tools out of bronze and iron.
( Bronze/ Iron Age blacksmiths, not primitive man)
Tubal-Cain's sister was Naamah."

A sister finally so where did all these women come from these Adamic men are hooking up with? Seems they find the more southern lands already populated in fact way over populated.

**Genesis 6 explains.**

" When human beings ( Aboriginals) began to increase in number on the land and daughters were born to them, the sons of Adam ( First Caucasians) saw that the daughters of humans were beautiful, and they married any of them they chose."

Caucasian (White) Man have a only 8000 years in Human History
The Iron Age is an archaeological era, referring to a period of time in the prehistory and protohistory of the Old World (Afro-Eurasia) when the dominant tool making material was iron. It is commonly preceded by the Bronze Age in Europe and Asia and the Stone Age in Africa, with exceptions.

Ancient iron production did not become widespread until the development of the ability to smelt iron ore, remove impurities and regulate the amount of carbon in the alloy. The start of the Iron Age proper is considered by many to fall between around 1200 BC and 600 BC, depending on the region. Then, the first farmers from the Near East arrived in Europe; they carried both genes for light skin. As they interbred with the indigenous hunter-gatherers, one of their light-skin genes swept through Europe, so that central and southern Europeans also began to have lighter skin. The other gene variant, SLC45A2, was at low levels until about 5800 years ago when it swept up to high frequency.

# The Beginning- Undeifying Creation טֶבַע

In the beginning nature created the heavens and the earth. Now the earth was formless and empty, darkness was over the surface of the deep, and the Spirit of life (יְהוָה) was hovering over the waters. And nature said, "Let there be light," and there was light. Nature saw that the light was good, and nature separated the light from the darkness. Nature called the light "day," and the darkness nature called "night." And there was evening, and there was morning—the first great cosmic geological era.

**And nature said**,

"Let there be a vault between the waters to separate water from water." So nature made the vault and separated the water under the vault from the water above it. And it was so. Nature called the vault "sky." And there was evening, and there was morning—the second great cosmic geological era.

**And nature said**,

"Let the water under the sky be gathered to one place, and let dry ground appear." And it was so. Nature called the dry ground "land," and the gathered waters nature called "seas." And nature saw that it was good. Then nature said, "Let the land produce vegetation: seed-bearing plants and trees on the land that bear fruit with seed in it, according to their various kinds." And it was so. The land produced vegetation: plants bearing seed according to their kinds and trees bearing fruit with seed in it according to their kinds. And nature saw that it was good. And there was evening, and there was morning—the third great cosmic geological era.

**And nature said**,

"Let there be lights in the vault of the sky to separate the day from the night, and let them serve as signs to mark sacred times, and days and years, and let them be lights in the vault of the sky to give light on the earth." And it was so. Nature made two great lights—the greater light to govern the day and the lesser light to govern the night. Nature also made the stars.

Nature set them in the vault of the sky to give light on the earth, to govern the day and the night, and to separate light from darkness. And Nature saw that it was good. And there was evening, and there was morning—the fourth great cosmic geological era.

**And nature said,**

"Let the water teem with living creatures, and let birds fly above the earth across the vault of the sky." So nature created the great creatures of the sea and every living thing with which the water teems and that moves about in it, according to their kinds, and every winged bird according to its kind. And nature saw that it was good. Nature blessed them and said, "Be fruitful and increase in number and fill the water in the seas, and let the birds increase on the earth." And there was evening, and there was morning—the fifth great cosmic geological era.

**And nature said,**

"Let the land produce living creatures according to their kinds: the livestock, the creatures that move along the ground, and the wild animals, each according to its kind." And it was so. Nature made the wild animals according to their kinds, the livestock according to their kinds, and all the creatures that move along the ground according to their kinds. And nature saw that it was good.

**Then nature said,**

"Let nature make mankind in our image, in our likeness, so that they may care over the fish in the sea and the birds in the sky, over the livestock and all the wild animals, and over all the creatures that move along the ground." So nature created mankind in nature's own image, in the image of nature created them; male and female nature created them. Nature blessed them and said to them, "Be fruitful and increase in number; fill the earth and care for it. Care over the fish in the sea and the birds in the sky and over every living creature that moves on the ground."

**Then nature said,**

" Nature gives you every seed-bearing plant on the face of the whole earth and every tree that has fruit with seed in it. They will be yours for food. And to all the beasts of the earth and all the birds in the sky and all the creatures that move along the ground—everything that has the breath of life ( יְהוָה) in it—Nature gives every green plant for food." And it was so. Nature saw all that nature had made, and it was very good. And there was evening, and there was morning—the sixth great cosmic geological era."

The six great epochs of creation listed by science agrees--
Once a understanding of just a few key words the Ancient meanings start to come into focus for instance the word, " Day" is more correctly translated as, " Epoch" The key here is knowing that the ancient Hebrews believed in a invisible creative spirit that exists in all of nature. Ancient Hebrews did not actually have any concept of a deity of any physical form. What is somewhat amazing is how much the ancient concepts of creation actually agree with modern scientific evidence, For instance , In my " Day" Men went to the Moon. While in God's, " Day " the universe is born, and dies. How long are these Days? The Sun orbits the galaxy In twelve huge epochs of time as we are now entering the age of Aquarius. " And there was evening,( Ice Age ) and there was morning ( Global warming ) —the eighth day.

## A Border Less Planet

We are all, Earthlings the same tribe. The Human Farms have separated us peoples into camps that war against each other for profit but in the end only Earthlings remain and the fences a illusion. Do away with all nations and religions and borders and you will still find we are all still here the same humans as we have always been the same always and with this new found peace our Great Mother suffers less. There is still a tree in the middle of Eden still full of fruit uneaten, a tree of life, shame the humans still divide this false world into- Good and Evil, Legal and Illegal, Right and Wrong, Truth and Lies, Light and Darkness, when in fact none of these things ever existed in nature and never will, only in the imaginations of false worlds created by man full of pollution, disease, war, greed, and corruption do you find these.

**" Wake UP! "**

See the Earth as it truly is a beautiful heavenly paradise floating among the stars. We are all born into heaven not the other way around, yet some still choose to make this place hell.

**Deuteronomy 30: 19**

" I call heaven and earth to record this day against you, that I have set before you life and death, blessing and cursing: therefore choose life, that both thou and thy seed may live:" -

The word, " heaven " as defined by the ancients is simply a planet with a breathable atmosphere that can sustain life.

We no longer run on horse power any more nowadays it's called petrol chemicals. Crude black gold the main source of this madness as so called energy companies scour the last remaining pristine areas of the planet for this stuff, while non horse powered combustion engines await by the billions. Yes, we know your Madmax motor is rated in horse power another great illusion a deception just like hot dog isn't dog, and hamburger isn't ham, and Parkay isn't butter. We have inherited a artificial world that is run by artificial intelligence, unplug from the matrix for once just once and see what is truly left of our natural world. The city limit sign failed now all the country is covered as the mega city plows the human race cows. The current so called powers that be have used divide and conquer as a means of controlling the masses of human beings for thousands of years but we are entering a age when men and women will no longer be divided or conquered but instead we have entered the Age of Aquarius. A new age of light and energy has dawn while Earthlings everywhere awakens, the nightmare illusion vanishes.

Well Okay some history-- When Moses made his exodus from Egypt with all the Hebrew Israelite tribes, he wandered in the wilderness for 40 years training his troops then his Kin, took the Canaanites by storm invading every city and conquering their lands leaving all dead even women and children in their wake at the command of a God. My Oh My, how things have changed?

Oh not to mention the conquest, Manifest Destiny held that the United States was destined—by God against the Native Americans a bit over a century back on the same note where millions in 380 some odd tribes eastward were reduced to a few thousand on reservations in the deserts of Oklahoma. Human history is riddled with border crossings of all kinds most are not very pleasant. Now Russia then the United States invaded Afghanistan after Iraq almost back to back sending millions of refugees into other counties with repercussions still on going and for what the opium and the oil resources ? Seems a bit strange that right after the US Military Forces gain the opium fields in battles with Afghanistans, a opioid epidemic breaks out in America a few years later. People really need to get better at connecting these dots cause, yes these problems go way deeper than anyone could ever imagine. The United States southern border problem? The best way to help these countries is already long past, that would of been to leave them alone in their native states, self sufficient in tribes instead of commercializing them into products of the state. The real reason the Cartels have grown so powerful in some of these Central, and South American counties is the demand for drugs or some other, " illegal " activity within America.The solution ? Basically learning to leave people alone in their own countries, stop exploiting their resources, for what ever reason. Shelter in place and begin this movement of self- sufficiency utilizing solar energy power stations, organic gardening, renewables, and electric vehicle technologies to all local areas, globally would be a good start. Ironically Germany is already a good example of this.

Artificial light, artificial flavors, artificial flowers, artificial fruit, artificial energy, artificial transportation, artificial sweeteners, artificial intelligence, artificial humans, artificial worlds, artificial religions, artificial fertilizers, artificial drugs, artificial insurance, artificial money, artificial animals, artificial houses, artificial water, artificial air, artificial blood, artificial heart, artificial weather, artificial thoughts, artificial gods, artificial borders - The adversary is the opposite of what is true and natural, some personify that adversary as Satan, Lucifer, The Devil, The Deceiver, The Evil One, The Fallen Angel, The Anti-Christ, The False God, or The Tempter, when in fact all these titles are artificial to the real artificial synthetic world that the so called Gods of this world are building around themselves all hybrid humans almost alien to our natural planet they are, but you can find them all doing what they do best selling you their artificial products with a Demon's smile. One man's good is another man's evil. One man's legal is another man's illegal. One man's right is another man's wrong. One man's truths are another man's lies. One man's light is another man's darkness, and visa versa. In nature there are no opposites just shades of the same thing, yet there is a balance within nature that strikes an accord with all living beings that seek the equilibrium within the spectrum of life's true eternal spirit.

What still amazes me is when the armies of men go about the country side murdering the tribes of men for what ever reason but mainly for exploitation there always seems to be a God involved to blame for the mass carnage. A God that is ultimately responsible for the acts of violent men to hide behind as if just a belief in a God makes it all okay to kill, maim, and murder when in fact in almost every case it is just the greed of men seeking resources of every kind to further their empires of mad illusions when true peace is as simple as laying down all arms of every kind forever.

" And Elo-Him Yod-Hey-Waw-Hey,( Creator of Natural Eden ) shall judge among the nations, and shall rebuke many people: and they shall beat their swords into plowshares, and their spears into pruning hooks: nation shall not lift up sword against nation, neither shall they learn war no more" - **Isaiah 2:4** ) "

## Why Colonizing the Moon Is A Bad Idea

The act of building anything on the Moon could alter its fragile delicate gravitation relationship with Earth resulting in massive alterations of weather patterns, ocean tides and seasons. Blasting things off the moon during the Apollo missions have already altered the Moon in many ways including producing a toxic atmosphere from alien gases not indigenous to the moon environment.. The Moon has served Earth well for billions of years just as it is so maybe we should just leave her alone.

Amazon CEO Jeff Bezos says,

" Colonizing the Moon Could Be the Key to Saving the Earth? "

What?

Humanities true survival is more dependent on decolonizing the mega cites of Earth, and moving all of humanity into more homeostasis environs in step with our natural evolution into the future, without all this madness, war, pollution, greed, borders, hatred, and religious, and governmental separations.

The real reason humans have not returned to the Moon is the dust..The dust on the moon is sticky very fine dust and is very deep and gets into everything and anything. You can't escape the dust on the Moon, so unless we can figure out a way to vacuum up all that dust no one is going to live for long on the Moon.

" The Apollo Moon missions of 1969-1972 all share a dirty secret. "The major issue the Apollo astronauts pointed out was dust, dust, dust," says Professor Larry Taylor, Director of the Planetary Geosciences Institute at the University of Tennessee. Fine as flour and rough as sandpaper, Moon dust caused 'lunar hay fever,' problems with space suits, and dust storms in the crew cabin upon returning to space. "

These spoiled billionaire geeks are already ripping this planet apart to make a buck, can't imagine what these Bozos' will do once on some other body in space. Pipe dreams and stupidity seem to go hand in hand with these guys. Like that Elon Musk guy blasting that car into space, as if there isn't already enough junk up there. I mean really ! What good is a car in space, when they are designed to roll on roads here on the Earth? Duh!

" Earthquakes, floods and other natural disasters could kill millions in the world's teeming "mega-cities" and time is running out to prevent such a catastrophe, a UN expert on emergency relief has warned.

In Kobe, a city which is still nursing wounds from the earthquake that struck a decade ago, the UN director of emergency relief, Jan Egeland, painted an apocalyptic picture of imminent natural disasters in the world's mega-cities, predicting they could be "one hundred times worse" than the Boxing Day tsunami.

"Perhaps the most frightening prospect would be to have a truly mega-disaster in a mega-city," Mr Egeland told the World Disaster Prevention Conference. "Then we could have not only a tsunami-style casualty rate as we have seen late last year but we could see 100 times that in a worst case," said Mr Egeland, who warned that "time is running out" to prevent such a catastrophe. "

" NASA scientists are also concerned about health issues that may result from inhaling Moon dust. When astronauts return to the Moon and travel to Mars they will have to be careful about what they inhale. In 1972, when Apollo astronaut Harrison Schmitt sniffed the air in his lunar module, the Challenger, he said that it smelled like gunpowder. His commander Gene Cernan agreed. "

Bottom line- We have plenty of problems to fix here on our, " Good Earth" first, rather than heading off into space to pollute, exploit and tear up some other world.

**Moon Colony Discussion-**

**Ron** - " Pretty much total nonsense...also, in the case of asteroid or runaway virus, we need a second population. Bezos is so right on this...although maybe for the wrong reason$ "

**Sol** - " The Moon has zero protection from anything flying through space such a cratered pitted dusty lifeless place where no current human being would ever survive much less want to live in a tin can. A asteroid shower would surly wipe out anything on the Moon first way before impacting Earth and as for a virus probably would start on the Moon and spread to the Earth."

**Ron** - " true...a proper moonbase would be below the surface, and very large. It would need to be self sufficient in energy, growing food, etc. A big job...but we should be getting on with it. Amazon just wants people there to deliver stuff to, but there are good reasons to do it. "

**Sol** - " Very Large? So you are suggesting millions of tons of extra mass on the Moon Plus thousands of rockets back & forth Madness total madness .. Not to mention excavating, displacing all that matter, MOON Matter mountain!` Humans been living on this planet and surviving for millions of years without living on the Moon so why now.. Why all of a sudden we must put humans on the Moon or we all gonna die! "

**Ron** - " Not at all...mine out the space below the surface using robots. Very large as in not a tin can... no lifting materials up from Earth...that would be insane. "

**Sol** - " There is not a lot of raw materials on the Moon for making shopping malls"

**Ron** - " Negligible change of mass, not that that has anything to do with anything. The whole thing about changes to the mass of the moon is nonsense...total, complete, nonsense. Check out what the mass of the moon is...human activity is not material. "

**Sol** - " A Mag 8 earthquake changed the whole orbit of planet earth just a few years back. So you think digging huge holes on the Moon wont have repercussions? Even a small impactor from space would totally destroy your underground base in a heartbeat.. Those things are not slowed down one bit by a atmosphere on the Moon. "

**Sol** - " We could create a 100 populations in space but if we don't change the warlike nature of the earthly humans we are totally wasting valuable energy and time, that could be spent here on the Earth creating a peaceful, Utopian Planet, with asteroid protection technology as well elimination of all disease, and sickness. Plenty to do here first just saying. And nobody has to live in tin can or in a hole in the ground "

**Sol** - " Actually the gravitational tug the Earth has on the Moon is not that strong, in fact the Moon is escaping Earth orbit and someday will simply just fly off on its own becoming another planet around the Sun, just saying we could hasten that day by jostling things around up there.. And knowing humans some explosions when war breaks out with the Moon Colonist when they want independence from Earth. "

**Moon's Surface**

With too sparse an atmosphere to impede impacts, a steady rain of asteroids, meteoroids and comets strikes the surface of the Moon, leaving numerous craters behind. Tycho Crater is more than 52 miles (85 kilometers) wide.

Over billions of years, these impacts have ground up the surface of the Moon into fragments ranging from huge boulders to powder. Nearly the entire moon is covered by a rubble pile of charcoal-gray, powdery dust and rocky debris called the lunar regolith. Beneath is a region of fractured bedrock referred to as the megaregolith.

The light areas of the Moon are known as the highlands. The dark features, called maria (Latin for seas), are impact basins that were filled with lava between 4.2 and 1.2 billion years ago. These light and dark areas represent rocks of different composition and ages, which provide evidence for how the early crust may have crystallized from a lunar magma ocean. The craters themselves, which have been preserved for billions of years, provide an impact history for the Moon and other bodies in the inner solar system.

If you looked in the right places on the Moon, you would find pieces of equipment, American flags, and even a camera left behind by astronauts. While you were there, you'd notice that the gravity on the surface of the Moon is one-sixth of Earth's, which is why in footage of moonwalks, astronauts appear to almost bounce across the surface.

The temperature reaches about 260 degrees Fahrenheit (127 degrees Celsius) when in full sun, but in darkness, the temperatures plummets to about -280 degrees Fahrenheit (-173 degrees Celsius).

The Moon has a very thin and weak atmosphere, called an exosphere. It does not provide any protection from the sun's radiation or impacts from meteoroids.

**Em Elle writes**,

" The Moon is a very special celestial body. It serves important functions such as controlling the rise and fall of the tides, and slowing the rotation of planet Earth. The Moon belongs to all of mankind, and no country can claim a celestial body as it's own for any use or occupation. All celestial bodies, including the moon, belong to the ENTIRE mankind of earth (1967 Outer Space Treaty). With the recent Moon landing by the Chinese space probe, is it not time that we began to ask some questions, such as "What gives anyone the right to probe and potentially violate our Moon?" or "Why is this even considered to be OK?" or "Is this not of some concern to us?" and even, maybe most importantly "Did we give our permission?". Very few places on Earth if any, remain untouched by man, the moon included. It would be nice to be able to just sit and look up at our Moon, our good old magical, mysterious Moon, and not to imagine there the presence of machinery, of mining, of man. It does, after all, belong to us all. Let it remain a much beloved mystery. So please, leave our Moon alone. It's not yours. "

**Sol -** " The Moon is one of humanities most sacred objects. It has been with us since the very dawning of our time here on Earth. For most of that time the Moon was our time piece in the sky, our calendar, our night light, our inspiration. For thousands of years humans have planted their crops in accordance with the Moon cycles, even the very menstrual cycles of the human female is linked to the cycles of the Moon. Not a single species of creatures on this planet can escape the influence the Moon has on them. All the oceans of Earth dance with the Moon with the ebb and flow of tides high and low. All forms of vegetation on Earth are tied directly to the light from that Moon. And now to think that a few people on our planet want to exploit that Moon for what ever reason is totally ludicrous, a selfish notion based on greed and ignorance. The good people of Earth must not allow this to happen. The good people of Earth must keep their Moon beautiful, sacred, unadulterated, pristine, and intact for all generations of humans to come on Earth forever. We declare our Moon off limits to human exploitation, mining and or colonization. We declare our Moon a international historic natural treasure for all mankind, and must remain in its natural state for all times future forever. "

## Solar Energy Equals Freedom

The " truth" always lies somewhere in the middle.. Truth is the use of fossil fuels on planet earth has caused a lot of problems. Truth is " socialism " along with many other forms of so called government has also caused a lot of problems including all parties. Solar energy is a personal choice. Electric transportation is a personal choice. Driving a souped up sports car that gets 3 miles to the gallon is a personal choice.. No government on this planet needs to get involved in this.. Truth is 8 billion humans can choose for themselves without any of this crap including Taxes, War or any other form of human degradation. In a truly free world Efficiency & Sufficiency & Sustainability rules and nothing else. The world dependent on steam for electricity ended with the advent of the photovoltaic cell. A silent solar revolution has occurred along with electronic efficiency, until at last the whole human race upon this planet Earth can free itself from metered electricity if it so desires the technology is sound.

Of course it takes a lot of electricity to make all this industrial crap no human being on earth needed just a few decades ago, truth is solar energy on the rooftop of a modest efficient family home will power that home for the lifetime of that home, without any monthly electric bills ever. Not only can that solar house power all the appliances and electronics within that home but can provide the electricity for electric transportation.

Sad how most of the monetary richest humans on this planet just don't get it, maybe they should take a course from millions of already existing off grid habitats about the globe already? Just consider one thing If humans embraced EV technology on a global scale with PV highway transit charging every single gasoline station on the planet would disappear along with all the electricity it takes to operate them, not the mention the energy to build and maintain all these things as cities are ripping up more trees to build more with acres of combustion engine car lots everywhere. 80 percent of all things manufactured are built to support that failed combustion engine automobile industry upon this planet. Start counting the auto parts stores, gasoline stations, new & used gasoline car dealerships in your town... et cetera just to name a few. Now multiply that by all the towns in the world not to mention the cities. Takes a lot of electricity to power all these useless skyscrapers all over the planet where corporate leaders sit in their ivory towers figuring out new ways to get more profits from all this madness they have perpetrated upon this polluted planet.

We see a fusion power plant everyday, it is the safe distance fusion power plant that every single human being on earth can tap into now for all their electrical needs. This power plant is 93 million miles away yet can deliver electrical power for all human power cells for billions of years into the future, and guess what this power plant will not cost humanity a single dime. You can generate a trillion barrels of oil, just like you can mine tons of uranium but if no human being on earth is buying it you go out of business. That is what is happening as billions of humans hook up to unlimited ultimate solar instantly renewable electrical power.

Nuclear Power has caused a lot of problems for places like Japan and still no real solution for the waste in America and elsewhere. Look at the big picture what did we use all that extra energy from the atom for, basically accelerated the destruction of this planet by expanding the cites to mega structures that now have the peril of our very planet hanging in the balance. This planet is ripe for earthquakes, volcano, hurricanes, you name it tsunamis, asteroid impacts. The biggest mistake with carbon is cutting trees and covering large portions of the planet with asphalt, instead of allowing the vegetation to grow instead.. Carbon is fine as long as you maintain the absorbents mainly forest, grasslands which are now urban sprawl. Electronics nowadays use little electricity, and appliances are super efficient, and wow! Insulation is mega fold better especially the foams .. and solar cells are getting dirt cheap and very efficient. What a waste of energy two ships passing in the night both full of solar cells heading to different countries, madness. Just allow each country to totally power all their homes with solar of their own makings then export. Our Sun is a normal star doing what stars do, mostly creating Light. I'd be more concerned about what all the crazed humans are willing to do to their own planet trying to make a buck instead.

We must declare an end to debt driven societies for starters. Electricity is light! Most human beings on this planet live in homes with roofs.. We have the technology now to turn that roof into a electric dynamo.. Edison never had this neither did Tesla yet both of them dreamed that someday this might happen. We all are that day. Solar Power uses Tesla's AC and Edison's DC. The trick is it uses both right over your head self -sufficient without any meters and soon without even wires as a truly wireless world emerges. Cost is relative, A so called Poor Man doesn't have as much stuff that needs electricity, thus, - A so called Rich Man might have dollars for uncontrolled electric bills galore. In the end both can afford what is needed it is just neither tries, well most. The Natural World was borne Solar Electric billions of years ago, seems just the Human Species has to play catch up. I would be slow to title this movement as " Socialist " Capitalist or any other human definition of a political party. If it turns out to be a bad way to produce electricity then its a bad way, Time will always tell, as lightning flashes and thunder rolls.

## Altered Timeline

The current system has not only wrecked our natural environment but has also altered the composition of the atmosphere until our whole planet is in jeopardy of a run away greenhouse effect that has already reached a tipping point. Human mega cities cover the planet like a cancer so yes the whole system needs rebooting in an entirely different way or our planet could lose it's life sustaining ability altogether. Infrastructure is obsolete already without advanced technology transportation systems, and the economy is based on the old feudal system since Roman times, not to mention the fossil fuels. Taxes are only fueling this madness at the cost of the labor of a people that really do not have a clue that they have financed the very monster that has been killing them from poison food, to corporate wars, to mass pollution of a planet. Give people all they earn so they can build a better world around themselves a more self-sufficient world where each person is a solar powerhouse. Millions are dying in hospitals everywhere from the diets of poison foods causing all kinds of disease, thousands are dying in car wrecks, thousands are dying from drugs mostly pharmaceuticals, not to mention the thousands that are dead from gang related killings, or religious fanatics, where yes people just walk right up and kill you. Yes, we need better Earth to Human relations as well Human to Human, or as you say we probably will not make it. Most of the taxes go to the war machine effort, the rest goes in payroll for this massive population that is dependent on that government check, from the salaries of the generals to the salary of the politicians to whatever. The roads are all falling apart because some fool has been running millions of these huge diesel trucks on the highways instead of lightweight self charging solar electric vehicles. Commerce is moving through the internet, and delivery is autonomous electric vehicles, and flying machines that don't need roads. The slavery must end.

A well educated self-sufficient DIY society will not need as much stuff moved about the globe whereas most is total junk that ends up in landfills anyway.. The photovoltaic road wireless charging will become the batteries as the intelligent solar cars and light trucks will be more like magic carpets that simply glide over the planet to any geographical location at ease without combustion of any kind. Think Amazon and Solar Powered Drones already a viable delivery system. The Earth itself will demand what it will take for the human race to survive, all we have to do is listen then adapt.

## Humans are attempting AI Future!

We Here! Humans are attempting to invent a future based on some form of technologies they believe may manifest, truth is no one can predict the future for there are millions of variables to consider. ( For instance a asteroid strike, a mega earthquake, a super volcano, a nuclear war, biological outbreak, invention...etc ) The pioneers of early america could have never foresaw such a future as we term as a now for instance. Status quo we are always living in someone's future from all the so called , " NOWS " of the past. Time Traveller's Dream which future will we travel towards today? We live within a time continuum that is expanding with the universe as all other divisions of time are an illusion just as all concepts of a future are an illusion, a vision in our minds projected as thought into the next second of future time. The future of some tribe still living in the jungle of the Amazon will be much different than a family living within New York City. Truth is future is relative just like time as it is what ever we make of it. So invest your time wisely towards the best future you can imagine.

## Its Alive

Each day I feel we humans of this Earth are edging towards a major event that will change each and every living breathing person of our species in a very profound way... "What I am speaking of has nothing to do with religion, science or technology, but instead the very nature within the very consciousness of our native Earth herself.

" ITS ALIVE! A Thinking ! Breathing Organism! She Knows..."

Mrs. Terra Earth, has basically used the ingenuity of the collective human species to build for itself a external nervous system, for lack of a better word we humans still call it the World Wide Web (Internet ) in all its various forms.

The Grid as a metrics is evolving, and will leave most so called , " Utilities " standing in the dirt, but hey, what is wrong with, DIRT? " More precisely: that about one billion years after it's formation, our planet was occupied by a meta-life form which began an ongoing process of transforming this planet into its own substance. All the life forms of the planet are part of Gaia. In a way analogous to the myriad different cell colonies which make up our organs and bodies, the life forms of earth in their diversity co-evolve and contribute interactively to produce and sustain the optimal conditions for the growth and prosperity not of themselves, but of the larger whole, Gaia.

That the very makeup of the atmosphere, seas, and terrestrial crust is the result of radical interventions carried out by Gaia through the evolving diversity of living creatures. Encountering the Earth from space, a witness would know immediately that the planet was alive. The atmosphere would give it away. The atmospheric compositions of our sister planets, Venus and Mars, are: 95-96% carbon dioxide, 3-4% nitrogen, with traces of oxygen, argon and methane. The earth's atmosphere at present is 79% nitrogen, 21% oxygen with traces of carbon dioxide, methane and argon. The difference is Gaia, which transforms the outer layer of the planet into environments suitable to its further growth. For example, bacteria and photosynthetic algae began some 2.8 billions of years ago extracting the carbon dioxide and releasing oxygen into the atmosphere, setting the stage for larger and more energetic creatures powered by combustion, including, ultimately, ourselves. The Gaia Paradigm - Describes a productive confluence between scientific understandings of Earth as a living system with cultural understandings(ancient and new) of human society as a seamless continuum of that system. More than one astronaut looking back at our planet has been awed into concluding that this blue and green globe is, in fact, a living being. Of course, many native peoples the world over have always believed and functioned on the premise that the earth is alive.

## All encompassing

Most industrialized human beings are so culturally brainwashed they cannot grasp the magnitude of the problem much less the magnitude of the solution. " All encompassing " Just people dumping a ton of money into government coffers to fund all these failed programs that do not educate people, and do not innovate our energy systems, or even advance the human race towards a sustainable future is not always the answer. In fact in most cases just feeding the fire of this continued corrupted and greedy mafia styled polluted system.

We can change our homes, our gardens, our lawns, our cars, our energy sources, our minds. But changing others is a grander challenge, but setting a example in our own backyard with greater stewardship would also be a great start.

It could be that it is way more important what one does outside the system than what one does inside the system. Sending thousands of people into a broken system just adds to the overall brokenness of that system. The very way the human family as a species lives upon this planet has to change towards a more coexistence with our natural world or it could be that the total extinction of the human species will become inevitable. "Getting out and registering people to vote and make every effort to encourage them to get to the polls, even carpool if you would like and get out the vote. Getting Candidates in office that have smart Innovative Ideas that Inspire people to do the same and having the Integrity to always fight corruption wherever they may find it is how the system can begin being healed." "Getting out ? " when people need to be staying in fixing up their own homes, - " even carpool? " Only adds to over congested petrol-chemical polluted highways.- " Getting Candidates in office ? "

Energy hog obsolete government buildings are a major load on existing electrical grids. " fight corruption? " - We are not at war with ourselves.. Corruption? Really the very nature of the current system is corrupt..The way the bitcoin so called crypto-currency market works is almost identical to the stock market. You got all these crooks sitting up these programs then they hold millions of whatever coin is launched for themselves, then when some fool comes along and puts in their hard earn money these crypto geek crooks cash out their free gotten coins to siphon off the cash. In the case of the stock market all these crooks start a company and set aside millions of free stocks for themselves and their buddies then place it in the public arena. When a bunch of fools come along to invest their hard earn money the stocks rise then the crooks cash in their free gotten stocks thus running off with all the money. Sad case as both just needs shut down eternally for whole the human race would be much better off without these racketeers. ( Not to even mention the IRS one of the largest mafia styled organizations on the planet illegally perpetrated onto the American people. )

The powers that be try to hide this fact with layers of smoke screens, endless rhetoric and total bullshit, but as more and more people wake up the truth shines into their dark corridors of filth, greed and deceit. In any attempt to actually try to save the world we may indeed actually lose it. Sometimes it is what you don't have to do today, not what you do that matters.

At ease, For instance,

" I need to go out and buy that electric car? "

No, you need to stay home and start that garden. " Energy isn't the problem, it is what humans are doing with the energy that is the problem. Should humans create more energy? With the current lousy track record with humans and energy use, probably not. There is plenty of energy in fact just solar energy could supply all of humanities electrical needs easy, but when you factor in all the extra junk humans manufacture with energy yes such a wasteland of endless crap.

We, " Humans" take a lot things for granted about our Earth. Earth like planets as we are finding out are very rare out there among the Stars. Yes, we know all about Drake's famous equation, but I for one am not buying it. After all what does it matter if the Universe is teeming with life, when it is what one particular species does on one particular planet that matters. So we must imagine as if we are it. We are the only planet in the whole Universe where life has evolved. Okay, more, how sacred is that? What an awesome responsibility. Well it would be a darn shame if this planet earth is truly the only place where life has evolved like this, yet can one species blew it for all the rest? From that perspective, we have to do all we can to preserve this planet with all of it's pristine nature intact, not just for the future generations of human beings, not just for all the future generations of all the other species that, home here to, but as a testament to the Universe as we all cry out, " We Are Here ! "

                    Happy Holidays Always
                    All Be Safe